An Appetite For *Lombardy*

CHRISTINE SMALLWOOD

An Appetite For *Lombardy*

The People, The Places, The Food

Photography by Daniel Bone

Research and author: Christine Smallwood

Jacket and book design: Anita Mangan

Inside cover map: Encompass Graphics

Specially commissioned photography: Daniel Bone

First published in the United Kingdom in 2016 by:

Bonny Day Publishing Limited, London

British Library Cataloguing-in-Publication Data

A catalogue record for this book is available from the British Library

ISBN 978-0-9550058-3-1

Printed in England by Gavin Martin Colournet

Recipes

The recipes in this book are those of professional, busy working chefs. We have tested them in home kitchens and amended them so that they work with domestic equipment and with more suitable quantities. There are inevitably some changes to the recipes but we have done our best to stay true to the spirit of the original while making it possible to replicate at home. Some are more assemblies of ingredients but give a good idea of the produce served in that area. However, to taste the dish in all its glory, nothing can beat going to the restaurant and eating it in situ.

Many of these chefs rely on taste, sight, instinct and experience more than written recipes, and all would encourage you to do likewise and have fun with your own culinary creativity.

Be sure to assess the risks of eating food such as raw eggs or beef or any ingredient that could potentially cause a health problem. You should also be careful when reheating or reusing cooked food.

Food photos

All recipe photos were taken on location in the restaurants where the dishes were prepared and as they were served. No stylist was involved and no special effects were used.

Inclusion

No payment has secured an invitation to participate in this book; inclusion could not be bought and the publisher did not pay anybody to take part.

Contents

Introduction

Many people have preconceived ideas about Lombardy: the economic powerhouse of northern Italy, the home of trendsetting Milan or the place where you can find such upmarket holiday destinations as Lakes Garda, Maggiore and Como (a certain Hollywood A-lister hasn't harmed the latter's reputation).

What fails to spring immediately to mind is the excellent food of this varied region. But it should. Yes, Lombardy is blessed with wonderful plains, lakes and mountains. But it offers some equally extraordinary food and wine.

There are, for example, exceptional cheeses such as Gorgonzola, Bagòss di Bagolino, Robiola and Bitto Storico. Bitto Storico in particular not only has a Slow Food Presidium, but is also the object of one man's battle to safeguard the continuity of a cheese that he considers to be as much a cultural statement as a dairy product. Then there's a regional tradition of rice and maize (the Lombards were — not always flatteringly — referred to as "polenta eaters") and lots of classic pastas, from buckwheat flour *pizzoccheri* to the filled *marubini* of Cremona and *tortelli di zucca*. Nor should you overlook the marvellous cured meats including bresaola and *violino di capra*.

Some classic dishes use prime cuts of meat such as *costoletta alla Milanese*. Others such as *cassoeula* are vehicles for less prized parts, perhaps pig trotters and ears. But both are regularly 'seasoned' with heated discussions as to the correct ingredients — and spelling. The sweet-toothed can find treats from Torrone di Cremona to Panettone di Milano. And you must try at least a few of the very good wines, many only known outside of Italy to wine experts.

Of course Milan is synonymous with fashion and design, while other Lombard cities have their own identifiers — Cremona and violins, Monza and the Italian Grand Prix — but alongside culture and sport, the foods and wines should be a major draw.

As should the Bernina Express (or Trenino Rosso — the little red train — as it's commonly known), which will give you a glimpse of a variety of breathtaking landscapes, from its departure down Tirano high street (literally) on its upward journey to the ski resort of St Moritz in neighbouring Switzerland.

The residents of Lombardy are hard-working and open to exterior influences, especially in Milan. As might be expected in one of Europe's major cities, fine and Michelin–starred dining is plentiful. However, many of these places already have high international profiles, so this book spends more time in the quality osterie and trattorie of the region.

Among these are places with a strong continuation of family history and traditions, such as Caffè La Crepa and Osteria Al Bianchi, although family involvement in Osteria della Villetta goes back further — to 1870. There are also those that began as simple family restaurants but are now better known for shining in the Michelin-starred galaxy: Ristorante Due Colombe with one star and Da Vittorio where the Cerea brothers have acquired a dazzling three stars.

Some osterie and trattorie have attracted those with experience from professions far removed from hospitality, such as all three siblings at Osteria del Treno. And there are lots of couples working together in places such as Erba Brusca, La Locanda delle Grazie, Sali e Tabacchi and Osteria dell'Orologio. And there's one owner whose decision to enter the professional kitchen was accidental, namely Paolo Reina at Antica Trattoria del Gallo.

There are also striking contrasts. The region's character is equally defined by large international names like Grana Padano (impossible to consider Lombardy without it) and small businesses such as the ancient rice mill run singlehandedly by Pietro Schiavi.

But regardless of where in the food chain these restaurants and companies are, they are all run by chefs and owners who are driven, hard-working, frequently uncompromising and lots of fun — sometimes all at the same time.

There are those who suggest that Lombard cuisine came about from a mix of two ingredients: poverty in rural areas and wealth in big cities where rich families' food was prepared by private cooks. Today, that state of affairs has evolved to an increasingly accessible choice between rustic simplicity and Michelin-starred dining. These, and all the stages in between, are distinguished by some of the most dedicated and enthusiastic chefs, managers and supporting staff you will ever meet. Who better to introduce you to some of the best current food and wine in Lombardy?

Ambivere

Between the bustling city of Bergamo and the tourist magnet that is Lake Como, Ambivere provides a moment of calm.

There are two theories as to the source of the town's name. One claims its origins are from Bergamo and that Ambivere is the dialectal modification of the Bergamasco word 'bevere', the plural of 'bevera', which means a small brook or stream. The second theory says that it has Celtic origins. Either way, nobody seems to want to argue about it, preferring to get on peacefully with their lives.

Trattoria Visconti
Fiorella and Daniele Visconti

via De Gasperi, 12
24030 Ambivere
T: +39 035 908 153
W: trattoriavisconti.it

Opening hours:12.30 –
14.30; 19.30 – 22.00
Closed: Tues and Wed
Holidays: last week of Feb
and first week of Mar

There's a smiling welcome at Trattoria Visconti from the first person you meet. However, it's not from your usual well-trained front-of-house staff member. In fact the smile is a bit fixed. The attire could do with an iron too.

But then who needs a smartly dressed scarecrow? Once you get inside the door, however, Daniele or his mother Fiorella will be there to greet you in a somewhat warmer, not to mention more conventional, way.

The scarecrows aren't simply there for decoration. Lots of produce for the kitchen is grown at Trattoria Visconti, overlooked by the campanile of Ambivere. As Fiorella Visconti explains, "The kitchen garden has the starring role here."

Her grandfather bought the building in 1932 and set it up as an osteria. She remembers doing her homework alongside diners and card players — and wine drinkers, who were the main clientele. In fact, back then, food was only served at weekends, bank holidays and weddings.

How things have changed. Today there's a menu full of traditional temptations including salumi and *casoncelli* as well as a vertical Bitto tasting, because cheese is a big love of Fiorella's. There's also far more than one white and one red wine to choose from these days. The list — overseen by Daniele — is predominantly Italian with a good Valtellina section and a small French choice. And it's pleasantly civilized; one feels better for being here.

But despite the fact that it is a lot more refined than the term trattoria may suggest, holding on to the old name was deliberate. Daniele explains that traditionally the word 'trattoria' in Italy "makes you think of places where

one eats typical things from the *territorio* in which one finds oneself. Then there are *ristorante* — but in recent years the difference isn't clear. When my grandfather began the business it was a trattoria. We kept the name for historic reasons and because we still serve food from our *territorio*."

And you can't argue impeccable provenance more convincingly than by pointing to your own plot of land. Even corn is grown here; it provides most — and some years all — of the polenta needed. It's then sent to be stone-milled locally at a place that Fiorella says "now uses electricity but used to be a proper water mill."

As a sort of insurance policy, a nearby farmer cultivates maize from the Visconti-grown seeds so in years when they run out, he can top up their supplies. And — in that way of people who have put down strong roots — they buy any additional fruit and vegetables from a local cooperative — one that trains and employs people with special needs to cultivate produce.

And when the weather's friendly, just sitting outside on the garden terrace, sheltered comfortably from the sun in an oasis of brightly coloured and fragrant calm, makes the food even better. Especially if you go for a wander around the edge of the vegetable plots to see what's flourishing — and perhaps say hello to the chickens.

Or try to identify the lesser-known wild herbs. Fiorella is very interested in these; when an expert confirmed that they had at least 20 edible varieties in

Above left: Fiorella and Daniele Visconti

the garden she found all sorts of culinary uses for them, in everything from jams to tisanes. More than a passing glance at the bookshelves will reveal some fascinating titles on the subject.

Daniele and Fiorella both speak English — Fiorella worked in London for a while in, confusingly enough, a Greek restaurant. Daniele's English comes from having studied finance at university. But he couldn't resist returning to the family business and staying near to the lakes where you'll find him wakeboarding whenever possible and of course involved in the wine world he adores.

As do his customers, helped by his lovingly organised selection and the setting in which it's served. In fact after a wine-enhanced lunch in the garden, sitting in the shade but feeling the gentle warmth of the summer sun, it's hard not to find yourself smiling as broadly as the scarecrows.

Polpettine di Zucchini
Courgette Polpettine

A family recipe from the 1940s that is still popular at Visconti today.

SERVES 4

2 shallots, chopped

Extra virgin olive oil, for frying

800g courgettes, finely chopped

100g breadcrumbs

100g Parmesan, grated

2 eggs

8 Amaretti biscuits, finely crumbled

Salt, to taste

Flour, for dusting

Handful of chopped parsley, marjoram and chives

Cook the shallots in oil until soft, then add the courgettes to the pan and cook for 15 minutes. Leave to drain in a colander and then transfer to a mixing bowl and add the breadcrumbs, Parmesan, eggs, Amaretti and salt to taste. Mix everything together, form 16 patties and lightly coat in the flour.

Pour enough oil into a non-stick pan to cover the bottom, then heat. Add the patties and brown them on both sides. Once heated through, remove and leave to drain on kitchen towel.

Serve hot or cold with a garnish of fresh herbs.

Wine suggestion: White – Lugana DOC, Cá Lojera (Trebbiano di Lugana)

Quaglia Selvatica Bergamasca e Polenta
Wild Quail with Polenta

Unsurprisingly, given that the corn is grown in the garden, polenta is a year-round favourite for Fiorella and her family.

SERVES 4

4 quail

150g sausage meat

Salt and black pepper

Small handful rosemary, finely chopped

150g pancetta rashers

A few tablespoons extra virgin olive oil

2 cloves of garlic

100ml white wine

Sprig of rosemary

Cooked polenta, to serve

Cooked vegetables, to serve

Clean the quail. Mix together the sausage meat, salt, pepper and rosemary and stuff into the quail. Place the pancetta rashers over the quail.

Pre-heat the oven to 180°C.

In a casserole dish, heat the olive oil with the whole garlic cloves over a gentle to medium heat. Brown the quails on all sides and pour over the white wine. Add a sprig of rosemary to the casserole dish and place in the oven and cook for about 30 minutes.

Serve with a spoon of the cooking juices, polenta and vegetables of your choice.

Wine suggestion: Red – Inferno Valtellina Superiore DOCG, Nobili (Nebbiolo)

Ristorante Macelleria Motta
Sergio Motta

strada Padana Superiore, 90
20060 Bellinzago Lombardo
T: +39 02 9578 4123
W: ristorantemacelleriamotta.it

Opening hours: 12.30-14.00;
19.00 – 22.00
Closed: Sun
Holidays: Aug

Some restaurant owners talk about the provenance of their meat. Sergio Motta is part of it. He buys the young animals at auction, oversees the raising of them by long-trusted *allevamenti* and then butchers them himself.

But then, he still sees himself primarily as a butcher. And if you didn't know the meaning of *macelleria,* and just stumbled upon his restaurant, the floor-to-ceiling cold store next to the entrance would give it away, packed as it is with carcasses and Parma hams hanging from huge hooks. Or you may be greeted by Sergio himself, manning the fireplace grill and perhaps showing a *costata,* a *filetto* or a *fiorentina* ready to be grilled to your preference.

But it's not just about the best cuts of beef, although they figure quite heavily. The main reason Sergio wanted to set up a restaurant was because he was finding it ever harder to sell certain parts of the animal in his butcher's shop in nearby Inzago. His intention was to serve heart, lungs and other parts that he was usually left with and show how good they are.

So he found a nearby restaurant on the market and a friend with the relevant restaurant experience. But the friend pulled out, and so Sergio decided to go it alone — against his wife's wishes.

It's amazing what a persuasive chat over a good cappuccino can do. His wife eventually came on board, adding her expertise to organise the interior decoration, which features, rather heavily it has to be said, photos of Sergio and large cattle, along with lots of award certificates and posters for livestock fairs.

He took over the shop in Inzago — also called Macelleria Motta — in 1993, thirty years after his father had set it up. The shop is now one of only two butchers in the town; the other specialises in pork. Sergio doesn't only sell raw meat but cooked tripe, and the popular *bollito misto.*

And in the restaurant, Mondays are *bollito* day. It's served proudly from a traditional trolley with a mix of *lingua*, *testina*, *coda*, *cappello del prete*, *biancostato*, *cappone* and *cotechino* with salsa verde and *mostarda di frutta*.

Sergio says he can't imagine doing anything else and his enthusiasm for meat — Bue Piemontese in particular — is unflagging (he goes regularly to Moncalvo in Piedmont to see the farmers who raise the cattle he buys). Ask him about the recent history of cattle breeding in Lombardy and the impact of heavy milk-producing strains. He knows his beef.

'Twas ever thus in his family, apparently. Even when his heavily pregnant mother told his father that their baby was on his way, the response was "but it's Saturday and there are lots of customers. Let's wait until tomorrow." Sergio arrived thirty minutes later.

When he was at school the highlight of his week was going to the cattle sheds on Sunday to choose an animal to butcher. On Monday afternoons he'd wash the young veal calves with a comb so that they'd be clean when his father butchered them. Now his young children are already dreaming about becoming butchers (except at weekends when the aim is professional football).

You won't be surprised to hear that Sergio is the most committed of carnivores. He eats meat every day, sees vegetarianism as a fashion and is adamant that it's not heavy meat consumption itself that causes health problems but bad quality meat.

"The reason people eat less meat these days is because many butchers and supermarkets sell meat which is too young," he insists. "It's too fresh so not tender enough. It's not just the cooking that is important; you have to be patient before that." Quality butchery: it's a lot more than slice and dice.

Above left: Meat and Sergio in his shop in Inzago

Above right: Sergio in the restaurant's cold store

Finissima Tartare di Bue Piemontese ai Tre Sapori: Naturale, con Olio e Sale, con Crema di Acciughe, Capperi e Tuorlo d'Uovo Intero
Beef Tartare Three Ways

Unsurprisingly, Sergio insists on Bue Piemontese for his signature dish tartare, and prefers "the tender leg meat".

SERVES 4

Salsa verde:
1 large handful of parsley, washed
5-6 anchovies in oil
60g capers
60g gherkins
½ small red onion
Extra virgin olive oil

Tartare:
600g tender beef, fat removed
Extra virgin olive oil
Maldon salt
4 egg yolks

To make the salsa verde, put all the ingredients, except the oil into a blender. Blitz and then pour the oil in gradually until you have a creamy consistency.

Chop the meat into very small pieces with a knife. Take 120g of the meat and form it into four equal balls.

Season the remaining 480g with oil and salt. Take 160g from this and form it into 4 separate discs. From the remainder, form 4 round discs of 80g each, pressing your fingers lightly into the centre of each to make a small indentation and then place an egg yolk on top.

To serve, place a spoon of salsa verde onto 4 serving plates and put the discs of tartare topped with egg yolks on top of these. Next add the 40g discs of beef seasoned with oil and salt to the plates followed by the unseasoned ball of meat.

Wine suggestion: Franciacorta – Brut Milledì Rosé DOCG, Ferghettina (Pinot Nero)

Gnocchi di Patate Ripieni di Ragù su Crema di Piselli e Polvere di Liquirizia
Potato Gnocchi filled with Ragù on a Pea Cream

An easy and filling recipe. This quantity will make about four gnocchi per person.

SERVES 4

Gnocchi:

500g potatoes, boiled, passed
  through a potato ricer (or mashed
  well) and seasoned

200g plain flour

250g sausages, oven baked and finely
  chopped

50g Parmesan

Salt and pepper to taste

Pea cream:

250g fresh peas

1 leek, finely sliced into julienne strips

50g butter

500ml vegetable stock

Olive oil, for frying

5g powdered liquorice (optional)

To make the gnocchi, mix the flour with the cooled potatoes and knead together. Roll out the mixture to approximately 4mm thick and cut out discs with a pastry cutter. An 8cm cutter should give you about 16. Place a small amount of meat onto each disc and close them up by pressing to form round balls.

To make the pea cream, cook the leek in butter, then add the peas and cover with stock. Cook for 10 minutes and then blitz until smooth. Keep warm.

Cook the gnocchi in boiling salted water for a few minutes, drain and then brown in a non-stick pan with a splash of oil. Serve immediately on the pea cream. Sprinkle over the liquorice powder if using.

**Wine suggestion: White – Herzù Langhe DOC,
Ettore Germano (Riesling Renano)**

**Red – CuoreDivino la Botte 18, Cabanon
(Cabernet sauvignon)**

Bergamo

The city of Bergamo has two parts: upper and lower. The Città Alta is reached by either a winding road or a funicular from the Città Bassa. The latter is well worth a stop but most visitors focus on the upper town with its bustling cobbled streets and hard-to-resist shops.

There's a good café at the top of the funicular and many nods around town to local composer Gaetano Donizetti. The Città Alta is also home to the noteworthy Piazza Vecchia. This is an architects' favourite; Le Corbusier declared it one of the most beautiful squares in the world.

Al Donizetti
Massimo Locatelli and Ornella Migliorata

via Gombito, 17/a
Città Alta,
24129 Bergamo
T: +39 035 242 661
W: donizetti.it

Opening hours: Sun – Fri
11.00 – 00.00;
Sat 11.00 – 00.30
Closed: Tues
Holidays: 25 Dec and
evening of 31 Dec

The patisserie is long gone, but the name of Pasticceria Donizetti is still on the outside wall of the building in all its typographic simplicity. Behind it, however, 17 via Gombito is now home to Al Donizetti, a much-loved wine bar which enjoys a stage set of an outside terrace on the main thoroughfare from the funicular to Piazza Vecchia.

The terrace used to house Bergamo Città Alta's covered market. Today it's the place in town for excellent informal dining with a range of not-easily-found-elsewhere wines.

Massimo Locatelli started running Al Donizetti ("it's a beautiful name, so we kept it") more than three decades ago. He'd studied electronics, so the hospitality business wasn't the obvious career choice. However, his teenage desperation to get together enough money for a third motorbike had led him to part-time work in bars and he gradually realised he wanted to stay in that field.

And then, as is so often the case, serendipity turned up — here in the form of his ex-girlfriend's father. A greengrocer looking for a new venture, he suggested they do something together. Massimo explained to him, "The only thing I know is bar work. Don't think that I can get to fruit and vegetable markets at four in the morning as that's usually when I go to bed." Thirty years on, Al Donizetti belongs to Massimo and his wife, Ornella.

Massimo retains some bar touches so you'll still find drinks such as Negroni, Bloody Mary, Americano, Campari soda and all the traditional *aperitivi*. And a well selected platter, perhaps bread, *culatello*, bresaola stuffed with goat's cheese and walnuts, Stravecchia, Robiola.

Above left: Massimo and Ornella

Above right: lunchtime service at Al Donizetti

Which offers just a hint as to the variety of cheeses, many from the presidia of Bergamo. And the province is not short of them: Agrì di Valtorta, Bagòss di Bagolino, Fatulì della Val Saviore, Stracchino all'antica delle valli orobiche. In fact there's a Bergamo saying: "*Lo bocca non è soddisfatto finchi non sa di vacca*" — which is a recommendation of cheese to end the meal, perhaps *tre stravecchi* (Bagòss, Castelmagno, *pecorino di fossa*) with a glass of Barolo.

The restaurant's excellent, unfussy meals are popular, but the highlight for many diners is the cheese and wine, both of which Massimo loves — as does Ornella, although she acknowledges that her husband's the wine expert.

The wine list at Al Donizetti has changed dramatically since 1990. That was the year when Massimo collaborated with the son of an *oste*, which meant the wines were taken more seriously. Today there's a large, predominantly Italian, selection. Massimo thinks the wines of Lombardy have significantly improved over the last couple of decades. When he started, he says, the focus was on neighbouring Piedmont, with a nod to Tuscany and a strong emphasis on Barolo, Barbaresco and Barbera.

But he realised that buying through wine reps meant that his wine list was identical to those in all the nearby restaurants. So he made his own discoveries. He's continued trying his best to go to vineyards and meet the winemakers. "We know about 80 per cent of the producers of our wines," he says. It's now a lot easier given that Lombardy is featuring heavily on the list, especially Franciacorta, which is a particular favourite. And Massimo is

keen to promote an ever-changing choice by the glass (as you'll realise from a quick glance at the blackboard).

As popular as the platters of quite extraordinary cheese and *salumi* are, some dishes are staple choices of the regulars, in particular the *casoncelli alla bergamasca* and the *lasagne al Taleggio (DOP) bergamasco* — and shaved truffles can be added when available.

The menu explains that Al Donizetti's suppliers are mainly small, artisan producers and that Massimo and Ornella pay particular attention to "products that hand down old flavours, our origins, culture and traditions." And that the staff share the Slow Food philosophy, encouraging diners "to stop hurrying, and enjoy your meal."

And they do. On a warm summer evening, diners look happy and relaxed, chatting to a background sound of gentle tinkling laughter and clinking glasses. In the winter everyone stays warm in the downstairs room.

The clientele is varied: local regulars, clued-up tourists, "all different types," says Massimo, "from the right to the left, from the young to the less young." Unusually for Italy, business is continuous. From 11 in the morning until midnight you can stop by for a coffee or something to eat and drink.

Above left: Heikki, one of the cheerful staff

Above centre: a glimpse of the terrace

Above right: Cakes and tarts including the Bergamo speciality of "polenta e osei"

However, it's no longer possible to reserve a table. It used to be but parking problems in the Città Alta meant that "we'd get shouted at by people waiting and by people who had booked but turned up 90 minutes late. So we thought, enough of that."

Which gives an idea of how popular, and how busy Al Donizetti is. It's hardly surprising that Ornella seeks some peace and quiet on her days off. "When I'm not working I like walking," she says, "but in silence."

Back on the buzzing Al Donizetti terrace, there's an impressive array of cakes (which nowadays come from a *pasticceria* run by a friend of Ornella's). The focus these days may be more on wine, cheese and *salumi* but excellent sweet treats still get a look-in. As does Massimo's electronics training. Well, sort of, "I'm well able to change the light bulbs by myself," he laughs.

Cocotte Speck e Asiago
Speck and Asiago Cocotte

At Al Donizetti they use a mix of half finely and half coarsely ground polenta for this recipe, but such a combination isn't essential. They cook and serve theirs in individual cocotte dishes, but this also works if cooked in one large baking dish and then divided before serving.

SERVES 4

500g polenta

Sea salt

300g Asiago, sliced (or substitute Branzi, Taleggio or Fontina)

150g speck

Cook the polenta in salted water according to pack instructions. Remove from the heat and leave to cool for 30 minutes.

Pre-heat the oven to 180°C.

Place a 2cm layer of polenta in an ovenproof dish or dishes, cover with slices of cheese and repeat finishing with bundles of speck. Place in the oven for 20 minutes or until cooked to your liking. Serve.

Wine suggestion: Red – Anrar, Andrian (Pinot Nero)

Lasagnetta al Taleggio
Taleggio Lasagne

Before Bergamo Alta's covered market closed and subsequently became the Al Donizetti terrace, the last stall holder standing was a cheese seller. So there's a pleasing continuity about Massimo still serving so many excellent cheeses on the same spot. Note that this recipe has a lot of cheese sauce so you may wish to reduce the quantity if you prefer a drier lasagne.

SERVES 8

500g fresh lasagne sheets

Salt

200g unsalted butter

120g 00 flour

2 litres full fat milk

500g Taleggio, skin removed, cut into pieces

Cook the pasta sheets in salted boiling water so that they are reasonably well cooked, softer than al dente (approximately 5 minutes).

To make the béchamel sauce, melt the butter gently in a pan, then remove from the heat and stir in the flour. Put the pan back on the heat and add milk gradually, stirring until everything has been incorporated. Mix in the Taleggio, stirring until you have a thick cheese sauce.

Pre-heat the oven to 200°C.

In a deep baking dish of approximately 30cm x 25cm layer sheets of pasta and then cheese sauce alternately until everything is used up. Finish with a layer of cheese sauce.

Put in the oven for 30 minutes, making sure that it doesn't catch towards the end. Cut and serve.

Wine suggestion: Red – Tiziano Merlot IGT, Colle dell'Aia, (Merlot)

Bianzone

Small and predominantly residential, Bianzone boasts some great views across the slopes of the Valtellina. Accessible from both the provincial capital of Sondrio and Tirano where the Bernina Express starts its journey to St Moritz, it's a convenient place to stay for visitors to the area.

It's quiet, but on a sunny Sunday morning a group of village friends are likely to be sharing a drink and joke at the bar marked 'Trattoria' on via Stelvio. Run by the imperturbable but accommodating Angelo, it occasionally issues a gentle but unexpected musical strain that may surprise you as you're passing by. Yes, that is the Grateful Dead.

Trattoria Altavilla
Anna Bertola

via ai Monti, 46
23030 Bianzone
T: +39 0342 720 355
W: altavilla.info

Opening hours: 12.00 –
14.00; 19.00 – 22.00
Closed: Mon (except in Aug
and on Bank Holidays) and,
from Nov to Easter also
Tues lunchtime
Holidays: variable

If ever a trattoria was a reflection of its owner, it's Altavilla in Bianzone.
Anna Bertola radiates from every corner, object and ornament. And there
are lots of ornaments. Lots. Some look as though they might topple over at
any moment. But these are not just trinkets; every one of them has a story.
Not that Anna will bombard you with these. No, she'll be far too busy
making you feel welcome.

Anna calls herself a '*locandiera*': an innkeeper. It's an old-fashioned word
but one that is appropriate here — not least because she runs a B+B above
her trattoria. "A *locanda* conveys a friendlier, more personal idea; it should
have a warmth that's missing from a hotel chain," she explains.

But behind the warmth is a rigorous approach to running one of the best
places to eat in the Valtellina. Go in the summer and eat on the terrace
with stunning views of the valley, or in the winter choose between the
traditional room and the new, modern one, which is dedicated to the
Valtellina and its wines.

She's proud of this room — and the wines it honours. As a sommelier,
Anna knows the winemakers well and loudly bangs the drum on their
behalf. That is one of the reasons why, when she had the shop at the side
of the restaurant converted into a room to help promote her *territorio*,
she also commissioned photos of some of them — to reveal the human
side to the bottles on display. She's a big supporter of the young
winemakers who are enthusiastically embracing the challenges of
cultivating grapes on these steep slopes, and she's thrilled about some
of the exciting things they're doing.

In fact you may well bump into one of them, either having a quick drink and a catch-up at the bar, or popping in to eat. You may also be fortunate enough to meet Anna's mother, a sweet-tempered lady who even now in her late 80s helps out for a couple of hours in the afternoon so that her daughter can have a short break. Of course when Anna's parents, both bakers, bought Altavilla, times were different. Back then you would regularly hear hushed tales of smugglers moving contraband over the mountains — a far cry from today's focus on walking and dining.

Although Anna had enjoyed helping out in the days when her mother ran the business, she left to study accountancy. She also took a fair few music lessons at the same time. Numbers and spreadsheets she now sees as necessary evils, but music is and always will be something she loves. There's a piano near the bar area with a big blues-inspired painting behind, and although Anna doesn't play very often, she has been known to have all sorts of people turn up with musical instruments and start a bit of a party.

She had wanted to study in Milan, but the objections of her parents — who saw it as a dangerous big city — put paid to that idea. So amid teenage grumblings she went the opposite way — to Alto Adige on the Austrian border. True to form (she's an optimist) Anna thinks that worked out for the best because it meant she speaks good German, which is very helpful these days.

Although many people come here for the well-executed traditional dishes on offer, her menu includes many other options because, as she puts it, "the locals don't want to eat *pizzoccheri* all the time; that's what they make at home." What they're definitely not going to have at home is the extraordinary selection of superb cheeses found here. Anna's a big cheese

fan — she's taken a number of courses — and enthuses, "I buy cheese with the maker's personality."

Which is why you won't find the non-local dishes to be 'international' food. "We started as an osteria, so people really shouldn't come here expecting to eat salmon and sea bass," she explains.

What you should expect, however, is some fresh produce from her small garden. Anna loves her garden and grows lots of herbs such as pineapple sage and valerian, as well as small supplies of salad leaves and physalis. And she's very particular about fresh flowers, explaining "When I see a restaurant with plastic flowers it makes me sad."

It's that constant attention to every detail and the enthusiasm that comes with it that bring people back again and again. So how does she keep it up? She thinks a bit, shrugs, and says, "It's something you either have, or you don't."

And she certainly does have it — in spades. "When I bring you bread, I'll explain what's in it, because you may not like all the different types," she says. "I'll explain the provenance of your oil because that's what should happen."

Not that she wants to be the one always doing the telling. "The great thing about Anna is that she listens," says a regular. And she does. "Not everybody wants to talk but when they do, it's wonderful to hear so many stories and get to learn about different lives and places," she says, adding, "Curiosity frees you; it enriches your heart and soul." Which may explain the quantity of trinkets and memorabilia dotted around. "They're things that I like: things that have come from my travels and are important to me." She points to a few items that are particularly relevant to her chosen career, saying, "The snails are the symbol of Slow Food." Well, most of them are. "I'm missing one that somebody walked out with."

But the great love in Anna's life is animals, and in particular, her adored dog Kira. It's hard not to fall in love with Kira yourself. She's the gentlest, most accommodating of pets; young children who have been to Altavilla clamour to play with her. Given her habit of sneaking unnoticed under the table beneath regulars' feet, it's not surprising that she's regularly trodden on by accident. But she never makes a fuss. Being a rescue dog from Naples, she probably can't believe her luck.

Is anybody ever disappointed when they come here? It turns out that some are just unrealistic. Somebody once complained that, despite all the photos he'd seen showing the terrace festooned with geraniums, there were none when he arrived. He came in November…

Travel up and down the Valtellina and, if you mention Anna to people, they'll smile and then affectionately tell you a story about something they once did together. Chances are that it'll end in uproarious laughter and a fond shake of the head.

Late at night, when the last few stragglers are lingering over their coffees, you may come across a group of villagers propping up Anna's bar while she dries glasses and tidies up. There's a strong chance that they'll all be enjoying a glass of fizz with her, and exchanging banter about a lifetime of shared experiences.

Names and words change but, as Anna says when explaining what she's aiming for, "In the past, osteria and trattoria meant something convivial and simple — a place with a heart that tells the story of its *territorio* with a warm welcome. You may like it, you may not, but my Altavilla is me."

Gli Sciatt con il Cicorino del Nostro Orto
Sciatt with Cicoria from our Garden

This is a classic dish from the Valtellina, using Casera DOP cheese which is hard to find outside of Italy. Substitute with Fontina (and Taleggio) if need be. Anna uses a 50/50 mix of coarsely and finely ground buckwheat flour, but this works with all finely ground flour too.

SERVES 6

250g buckwheat flour

150g white 00 flour

Salt, to taste

330ml light beer

200ml Nebbiolo della Valtellina grappa

Water, as needed

Pinch of bicarbonate of soda

250g Valtellina Casera DOP cheese – not too mature, cut into 2cm cubes

Oil, for deep-frying

Large bunch of cicoria, sliced into thin shreds

Extra virgin olive oil, for dressing

Wine vinegar, for dressing

Put the flours, salt, beer and grappa into a bowl and mix with your hand to make a batter. Add water to loosen slightly if need be, but the mixture should be quite thick. Leave this in the fridge for a good couple of hours.

In a high-sided pan, heat the oil to 190°C. Add the bicarbonate of soda to the batter. Put the cheese cubes into the batter individually and ensure that they are completely covered. Using tongs, remove the cubes one by one and drop them carefully into the hot oil. Move them around with a large perforated spoon so that they become brown all over and then remove from the pan. Place on kitchen towel to remove the excess oil and then serve on a bed of cicoria, dressed with oil and vinegar.

Wine suggestion: Red – Sotamà, Rivetti & Lauro (90% Nebbiolo, 10% Shiraz)

I Pizzoccheri alla maniera di Mamma Lucinda
Mamma Lucinda's Pizzoccheri

Anna uses delicious local mountain potatoes and serves very generous portions. You may well only require half of the quantity given here, unless you've had a particularly energetic day. Dried pizzoccheri are available should you prefer.

SERVES 6

Pizzoccheri:
600g buckwheat flour
300g white 00 flour
1 tsp salt
400-500ml water, as needed

300g potatoes, peeled and cut into cubes
150g Savoy cabbage, cut into wide strips
300g young Valtellina Casera DOP cheese or Fontina, thinly sliced
150g Parmesan, grated
½ white onion
150g butter
Salt and pepper, to taste

To make the *pizzoccheri*, mix the two flours and the salt together. Add the water and knead for about 10 minutes. Roll out to about 3mm thick with a rolling pin. Cut out lengths of about 8cm wide and then cut these widthwise so that you have tagliatelle of about 7mm wide

Cook the potatoes in salted water and after about 5 minutes add the cabbage. When the water returns to the boil, add the *pizzoccheri* and bring the water back to a gentle boil.

After about 10 minutes drain some of the *pizzoccheri*, potatoes and cabbage with a perforated spoon, placing them into a warmed baking dish. Place some slices of cheese on top, along with some Parmesan and then continue alternating layers of *pizzoccheri* and cheese.

Fry the onion in the butter and when browned, scatter over the top of the *pizzoccheri*. Serve on a pre-heated plate, with freshly ground pepper to taste.

Wine suggestion: Red – Carterìa Valtellina Superiore Valgella DOCG, Fay (Chiavennasca - Nebbiolo)

Borgonato

Borgonato is small and quiet but it does at least have a café should a morning coffee be needed when you are passing through.

Of course, being in the heart of Franciacorta, it's better known for harder-hitting refreshments: it may not be very big, but it's home to both the beautiful Berlucchi winery as well as the Borgo Antico San Vitale grappa distillery. Don't, however, be misled by the quantity of alcohol — this is a civilised place with polite and reserved residents

Ristorante Due Colombe Al Borgo Antico
Stefano Cerveni and Sara Magnacca

via Foresti, 13
25040 Borgonato
T: +39 030 982 8227
W: duecolombe.com

Opening hours: 12.30
-14.30; 19.30 - 22.30
Closed: Sun evening
and Mon
Holidays: first week of Jan,
and Aug

"Running a kitchen is like conducting an orchestra," says Stefano Cerveni, chef and owner of Due Colombe in Borgonato. But then he studied music for 17 years and was on the verge of playing professionally, so it's hardly a groundless comparison.

But when it came to choosing between a tuning or a serving fork, it was the kitchen cutlery that won the vote — thanks to a career-defining moment. "One day I cooked a dinner for some very important guests," he says. "I was under a lot of pressure to do something wonderful — and I did."

Having eaten, the group of very happy, contented guests appealed enthusiastically for Stefano to play the piano for them. "I felt the same intense pressure that I'd felt when I'd been cooking," he says, "but I played terribly. I realised that all of us have a predisposition for something, but when you have a genuine talent, then pressure brings out your best." Cooking, he decided, was the way forward. "Today I love playing the piano — but just for me," he says. "If I have to perform, I forget the notes!"

But he still likes to acknowledge his audience, so as a matter of course, he leaves the kitchen to personally welcome diners. "It's a simple courtesy," he insists. "If I want my guests to respect me, then I have to respect them."

But this courtesy led to a lot more than respect one night when he spoke to a table of three who arrived in a state of great excitement about their first dinner in a Michelin-starred restaurant.

Laura, the instigator of this night out, had seen Stefano on the TV and convinced her husband Andrea and her best friend Sara to go to his restaurant near to them in Rovato. They expected to have a great time but

didn't anticipate such personal attention — even extending to a very rare private piano recital by the chef himself after dinner. Sara in particular certainly didn't expect that. But then Sara also didn't expect to end up living with Stefano.

We don't know what Stefano performed that night. He loves jazz, ragtime and rock but can offer a wide-ranging mix of genres and foot tappers. Whatever it was, it clearly made a lasting impression as Sara subsequently moved house. In fact she ended up changing her job to work with Stefano. It was a very practical way of solving the problem of one partner working in a restaurant and never being around at the same time as someone with more conventional office hours.

Sara now does almost all the organising and managing so that Stefano can spend as much time in the kitchen as possible. Seemingly unflappable, it's her efforts that make everything look effortless. She takes great care ("we have to do all we can to bring people's dreams to life") of all the wedding receptions and big parties held in the stylish (deconsecrated) church that forms part of the restaurant. And understandably a lot of people choose to

Above left: Stefano Cerveni
Above right: The restaurant entrance

celebrate here. It's a calm space with a well-kept, clean and minimalist garden. It's easy to imagine elegant, long-limbed guests being languorously stylish over the chic lawn furniture.

Beyond the stone walls that surround the garden, the vines of Franciacorta are within touching distance. But even nearer — in fact right next to the lawn — is the grappa distillery: Borgo Antico San Vitale. For grappa novices who don't know their Grappa Franciacorta from their Grappa Franciacorta Barricata, a tasting session here would be a good place to start. It was certainly a good place for Stefano. The distillery owners, the Gozio brothers, approached him when he was running Due Colombe in the centre of Rovato to ask if he'd like to move his restaurant to share grounds with the distillery.

Stefano took over the original Due Colombe, which was set up by his grandmother as a simple trattoria, from his parents. Under his management it gained a Michelin star in 2008. Shortly after this he was on his way to Borgonato and the beautiful setting of the current Due Colombe.

It looks superb. The main dining room is light-filled and grand, albeit in a very understated way. It's been restructured simply and less looks as though it's cost a lot, lot more.

But then Stefano is good at concentrating on what's important and removing the inessentials. His signature dish, for example, harks back to his home town and is a — or rather the — Rovato classic, 'beef in oil', but in keeping with modern lifestyles and the resulting culinary changes, he's removed a lot of the oil. Don't expect to find floral arrangements on the table either. "I don't like flowers there," he says, "I prefer grissini." But if grissini are not your thing, rest assured that a home-made bread selection made with cereals and herbs will be served. And, of course, so will the Franciacorta. Stefano's so proud of the sparkling wine of his home region that he jokes, "My blood is bubbly."

And the fizz will be followed by some great food — some in creative recipes, some based firmly on tradition, but all in tune with his philosophy that what you cook is a reflection of your life — that, appropriately in his case, "composing a song is the same as composing a plate of food". Music's loss, Lombard food's gain.

Risotto Mantecato al Grana Padano, Ragù di Quaglia Sfumato alla Grappa di Chardonnay
Grana Padano, Quail and Grappa Risotto

It makes sense that Stefano includes grappa in some of his recipes, given that he shares his grounds with a distillery. He uses quail for this but it works very well with pheasant breasts too, should you have less time for preparation.

SERVES 4

Parmesan crisps (optional):
50g grated Parmesan
5g plain flour

Risotto:
1 shallot, finely chopped
50g butter
300g Carnaroli rice
125ml white wine
2 litres light meat stock
80g Grana Padano, grated

Quail ragù:
Diced meat of 2 quail
10g butter
1 sprig of fresh thyme
5ml Chardonnay grappa
10ml quail stock (made with the carcasses, vegetables, white wine and seasoning)
10ml rosemary infused olive oil

To make the Parmesan crisps (if using). Mix the Parmesan and flour and sprinkle in a thin layer onto the base of a non-stick pan. Place over a medium heat for a few minutes until the mixture is hot and similar to a crêpe. Flip it over and remove the pan from the heat. Leave to cool.

To prepare a classic risotto, lightly cook the shallot in 10g of the butter and add the rice to coat it. Pour in the wine, and cook by gradually adding the hot stock as required and continually stirring. Finish by mixing in the rest of the butter and the Grana Padano until the risotto is creamy.

While the rice is cooking, brown the diced quail with the butter and thyme over a high heat in another pan. Pour in the grappa, let it evaporate and then add the quail stock. Remove from the heat and mix well.

Divide the risotto onto 4 flat plates, add the quail ragù and its sauce, a few drops of the rosemary oil, break the Parmesan crisp into pieces over the risotto (if using) and serve immediately.

Wine suggestion: White – Curtefranca Bianco Uccellanda, Bellavista (Chardonnay)

Il Manzo all'Olio delle Due Colombe
Due Colombe's Beef in Oil

This is one of Stefano's signature dishes, based on the classic dish from his home town of Rovato. He uses a 2kg piece of cappello di prete in the restaurant, which serves 10, but this is a version for a smaller number of people.

SERVES 5-6

25g butter

2 salted anchovies, finely chopped

2 cloves garlic, finely chopped

1 small onion, finely chopped

1kg feather steak, cut in half
   lengthwise

1 tsp Acacia honey

2.5 litres boiling water

100 ml extra virgin olive oil

25g cornflour

10g fresh spinach leaves,
   very finely chopped

1 small boiled carrot, very finely diced
   (brunoise)

Cooked polenta, to serve

5-6 boiled potatoes, to serve

In a large saucepan melt the butter and gently fry the anchovies, garlic and onion. Add the meat and brown lightly on every side. Spread the honey onto the meat. Add the boiling water to the pan. Cook uncovered over a medium heat for about 3.5 hours. Skim off the impurities that float to the surface during the first 5 minutes.

Now add the oil to the water. Mix the cornflour with a small amount of cold water and stir in. Continue cooking for another 5 minutes moving the meat frequently but very gently, so that it doesn't stick.

Remove the meat from the pan and reduce the cooking liquid to a thick sauce. Add the spinach and carrot.

Serve the beef in 4-5cm thick slices, covered with the cooking sauce and accompanied by polenta and boiled potatoes.

Wine suggestion: Red – Pomaro Curtefranca Rosso DOC, Castello di Gussago (Cabernet Sauvignon and Cabernet Franc, Cabernet Carmenére, Merlot)

Brescia

The eyes of the car-loving world turn their focus on Brescia in May, when Mille Miglia frenzy takes hold. But with numerous artistic and architectural treasures — Palladio is partly responsible for the Palazzo della Loggia and the city houses the fascinating Santa Giulia Museum — there's plenty in this provincial capital for non-petrolheads to enjoy.

Every June Slow Food organises Brescia con Gusto, a vibrant evening food festival giving visitors and residents alike the chance to follow an established route around town, speak to local chefs and producers — and party with them.

Osteria Al Bianchi
Michele Masserdotti

via Gasparo da Salò, 32
25128 Brescia
T: +39 030 292 328
W: osteriaalbianchi.it

Opening hours: 09.00-14.00;
16.00-24.00
Closed: Tues and Wed
Holidays: 2 weeks either
side of Ferragosto (Aug 15)

Of all the social rituals in Italy, the *passeggiata* and end of day *aperitivi* are particular favourites. Ending either of them at a welcoming osteria is, as it were, the ice in the Negroni. Of course, it has to be a traditional osteria, a place where "ordinary people socialise and know they'll eat good simple food," as Michele Masserdotti, the driving force behind Osteria Al Bianchi, puts it — with a strong emphasis on the *"buono."*

And this osteria in the heart of Brescia is just such a place. The affable, convivial Michele, who took over from his parents in 2002, may always be ready for a party but he also has the necessary restaurateur's eye for detail. And a lot of energy, which you need when the Mille Miglia vintage car race drives into town. "We do 18 very busy hours a day for four days then," says Michele. "Without a break."

But then Michele's normal day isn't nine-to-five. Osteria Al Bianchi opens at nine in the morning for coffee but doesn't close until midnight, with just a couple of hours break in the afternoon. Pop in for a quick espresso at 10am (coffee only, no pastries) and don't be surprised to see men of a certain age, all spending the same amount as you are for a small glass of house wine.

But after that they'll take their time, read the local paper from cover to cover and gently catch up on the town's gossip with whoever else pops in. Then, in the predictable, timetabled way of Italy, the lunch crowd will arrive for a quick *aperitivo*. The pre-dining classic in Brescia is the *pirlo*, a simple combination of Campari, white wine and sparkling water, often with a shave of lemon peel, Michele serves his in small balloon glasses in the traditional way, refusing to upsize to a big glass *pirlone* with lots of ice like an Aperol spritz. Michele has no interest in bar and drink fashions.

Above right: Michele and some regular card players

Below right: The osteria's dining room

Nor in food trends. This sort of osteria is not the place for the latest gastronomic fusions and foams. The menu here always includes *stracotto d'asino*, *casoncelli* and of course the *malfatti*. Michele's *malfatti* are a big draw — not just for the locals, but for people who arrive from around the world to search them out.

And at lunchtime something rather wonderful happens. A mix of long-retired individuals, busy professionals and regular locals turns up. Lots of the elderly people have a dining ticket from the local council that entitles them to a simple meal from a limited but fresh and ever-changing menu. Many of them choose to share tables so they can eat and socialise with other diners. Yes, this is a private business concern but it's one with deep local roots and enough soul to remain truly inclusive, offering an unfussy, valued community service.

The oldest regular arrives when lunch has finished. He's 89 and comes from 1km away, travelling on either bike or foot. He walks past the bar to the back room. There, for a few hours in the afternoon, the emphasis changes. It's that card-playing time of day and drinks are permitted — but no food; it might mark the cards. From the bar, the mocking and banter in the back room can be heard, and loud bursts of drama as the tension builds. Oh, and along with no food, it's no women either.

Don't be dismayed. This isn't a male-only stronghold. But you may also notice that there are no female employees. There's a reason for that. "Brescia used to have lots of heavy drinkers. My parents decided to hire only men so that if things got out of hand, no women would be bothered,"

Above left: A Brescian *pirlo*

Above centre: Outside eating and drinking at Osteria Al Bianchi

Above right: The osteria's sign

Above left: Michele at the osteria's bar

Above right: The salumi store

says Michele. "We're a traditional place and so we've stayed the same." Mind you, Michele's mother used to work here for a while and what she lacks in size she makes up for in strength of character.

These days she only pops by to eat, whereas Michele's father, Franco, still does a few hours work here. "His heart would break if he couldn't come in to take the orders, because he still wants to be involved," Michele explains. It must have been hard for his parents, Franco and Cici, when they handed over to Michele, but he acknowledges that he's carrying on what they started. "My mother was the warm and welcoming one; my father was the worker. I gained the best from both of them."

Osteria Al Bianchi is one of those places that you wish you could transport to the corner of the road where you live. But of course you can't because it's not just the interior and the food, but the people — those who run it and those who come here, from the big characters to the small, from the quieter ones in the background who make up the chorus, to the scene-stealers.

But if you want to see even more Brescians at play in and around the Osteria al Bianchi, then drop in during the Brescia con Gusto festival. Michele loves this outdoor eating event, and always has a stand outside the osteria where he serves 250 portions of food and 250 glasses of wine to people who have bought tickets for the route he features on. "It's such a great occasion. It's a culinary party." So says the man you'll probably find still making merry with his mates at two in the morning, long after all the ticket holders have been served. There's no more fun-loving *oste* in Brescia.

Casoncelli alla Bresciana
Brescian Casoncelli

These pasta parcels are a local speciality and the simple addition of melted butter and sage leaves is ever popular. Michele's filling becomes a smooth paste due to how finely he minces his meats but if you are using less fine mince, compact the filling slightly so that it stays in the centre of the pasta to facilitate closing the parcels.

SERVES 4-5

Pasta:

330g 00 flour

3 large eggs

Filling:

160g finely minced beef and pork

30g salumi (such as mortadella and prosciutto crudo), finely minced

Olive oil for frying

65g Grana Padano, grated and extra for serving

20g breadcrumbs

Salt and pepper

Butter and sage leaves to taste

To make the pasta mix the flour and the eggs together and knead to a smooth dough. Cover and leave to rest for 30 minutes.

Fry the minced meats with some oil. Remove from the heat, add the cheese and breadcrumbs, mix thoroughly and season.

Roll out the pasta thinly, either with a rolling pin or with a pasta machine and cut into squares of 9cm. Put a small quantity of filling in the centre of each square and fold over to form a triangle. Press the edges closed with a fork.

Cook the pasta parcels in salted boiling water until done to your liking. When cooked, drain and put on a serving plate. Grate Grana Padano over them. Heat the butter with the sage leaves in a pan then pour over the pasta before serving.

Wine: Red – Groppello di Lago di Garda (Groppello)

Mousse allo Zabaglione
Zabaglione Mousse

This is a light, but rich dessert, so Michele serves small amounts in individual glasses. Do check the instructions of the gelatine you're using to ensure that the quantity is correct.

SERVES 20

9 egg yolks	25g pine nuts
125g caster sugar	90ml cognac
90ml Marsala wine	1 sheet gelatine
75g shelled almonds, finely chopped	500ml fresh cream
25g raisins	

Place a heatproof bowl over a pan of hot water. Add the egg yolks, sugar and Marsala and cook gently while stirring. When the mixture is pale and thickening stir in the almonds, raisins and pine nuts and then flambé with the cognac.

Add the gelatine to the mixture according to the pack instructions, and leave it to cool. Whip the cream to stiff peaks, and fold into the zabaglione. Spoon into individual glasses and chill.

Wine: Dessert – Passito Sole di Dario, Azienda Agricola Cantrina (Sauvignon, Semillon, Riesling)

Trattoria La Madia
Michele Valotti and Silvia Peroni

via Aquilini, 5
25060 Brione
T: +39 030 894 0937
W: trattorialamadia.it

Opening hours: Wed – Fri
19.30 – 22.00; Sat 12.30 –
15.00, 19.30 – 22.30; Sun
12.30 – 19.30
Closed: Mon and Tues
Holidays: one week in Feb
and one week in Aug

"It's a person's flaws that interest me," says Michele Valotti, chef and
co-owner of La Madia. "Flaws are interesting. They create anticipation.
When you buy a cheese from the supermarket, you always know what to
expect. It's always the same. It's standard. But it should have defects: a
mark, more of one thing or another. It's this aspect that produces a moment
of magic when you cut into it."

Michele Valotti, chef and co-owner of La Madia, sees such imperfections as
a particularly attractive part of small-scale food production, and is
fascinated by the stories of individual food producers. He's certainly quick
to underline their importance, a tendency neatly summed up by some
words you'll find painted on one of the dining room walls: "Behind our
food are not brands but faces."

And some 20 years since he and Silvia Peroni left the *agriturismo* they were
managing and set up La Madia, he's become ever more committed to this
approach. He articulates his beliefs clearly, at times almost poetically — but
then he is a philosophy graduate.

"Whether you enjoy a plate of food or not, there's always a story and a
world behind it," Michele says. "I don't think we should say, "Don't go to
McDonald's because it's not '*buono*.'" Some people think it is. We should
look beyond the idea of '*buono*' at what's behind the food served. We try
not to add unnecessary things — we make a pear sorbet from the farmer's
pears. Full stop. We don't add any flavours or concentrates. If you only
think about whether it tastes '*buono*' or not, you end up with a palate that
has been trained by additional ingredients — often just chemicals." He

adds, "The cheese here is wonderful — and when I say cheese, I mean cheese made from raw milk."

Not that he sees himself as an educator on taste. "I don't believe this is education but communication," he insists. "I'm just giving people tools to choose their own direction."

You don't have to be quite so serious-minded to eat here, though. Even Michele, who takes his job very seriously, loves to wear bright colours and is fun enough to have a hard-working yet cheerful team around him, led of course by Silvia who runs front of house and has an endless supply of smiles and warm welcomes.

Silvia may pour you an *aperitivo* (the bottles of the secret house mix have charming hand-drawn labels) while getting a bowl of water for someone's dog. She calmly explains the more unusual things on the menu, even if she's run off her feet in the middle of a packed service. Things like (an occasional daily special) *La Zuppa del Raccoglitore*, named after the young guy who goes out and gathers the wild herbs for La Madia. Or carrot *gnudi*, vivid orange "ravioli insides without the pasta", with splashes of a glossy green pesto of carrot tops. Or the one constant on the menu: *Spiedino di pollo nostrano e biologico*, a chicken kebab served on a large metal frame, with an advance warning that it takes a while to cook because this was a chicken that

ran around looking for food. "I think that our chicken in its simplicity is truly an authentic food," says Silvia, "but so many people have never eaten a chicken like it so we need to explain."

And all the well-trained staff are equally engaged and informed. Occasionally a chef will appear from the kitchen and serve what they've cooked. Together they make up a happy, efficient team that understands what makes La Madia different and can talk at length and in depth about the menu. It's impressive.

As is the car park, albeit for somewhat different reasons. La Madia isn't really a passing trade place. It's high up on the outskirts of tiny Brione, with its few hundred inhabitants. To enjoy the restaurant and its view over Franciacorta and the province of Brescia involves an uphill drive along winding roads. Which is why all space in the car park is precious — and yet everyone obligingly parks in jigsaw formation and graciously moves when asked.

Not that diners are rushed to leave once they're seated — seated at tables that are reliable and cared for but worn. The integrity-laden food served at La Madia belongs on these tables. As it belongs among all the old items that decorate the dining rooms. But then Michele rather likes aged things. "They have a story and something old makes you think of all the people who have used it. I find that fascinating." That and The Beatles, ("a religion since my teenage years") as you may find out when you visit.

There's a lot of concern about food sourcing but also a sense of cheer about La Madia, helped, of course, by those bright colours Michele enjoys so much. "The world is full of colour, so why does everyone buy grey things?" he asks. "I've never seen a field of grey flowers."

That glossy green carrot top pesto perhaps sums up La Madia's combination of vibrancy and integrity. It may be a great use of all ingredients but to Michele it's not an economic consideration but a cultural one. "We've forgotten that these parts of the plant are edible because they're usually sold without them," he explains.

With his quiet, calm authority, and Silvia's able, warm assistance, Michele will whisper his words of wisdom and change that, one forgotten veg part at a time.

Tagliolini con Tonno di Coniglio e Tonno di Tinca
Tagliolini with Rabbit and Tench

La Madia's tagliolini recipe contains both meat and lake fish, such as tench. It works well with river trout too.

SERVES 4-5

Pasta:

350g organic semolina

150g organic white 0 flour

Pinch of salt

4 medium organic eggs

75ml water

150ml of walnut or other nut liqueur, heated to remove alcohol

30g rabbit per person (any part of the rabbit meat will do)

1 bay leaf

Extra virgin olive oil,

30g cleaned fish per person, cut into medium sized pieces

Vegetables:

100g of mixed courgettes, carrots and asparagus per person, cut into fine strips

Extra virgin olive oil

Salt, to taste

50g cherry tomatoes per person, halved

Handful of thyme and mint, chopped

Breadcrumbs:

Handful of breadcrumbs

Extra virgin olive oil

1 clove of garlic, finely chopped

Salt

Handful of parsley, chopped

To make the tagliolini, mix the pasta ingredients together and knead to a fine dough, then roll and cut with a pasta machine. Alternatively, use ready-made long, thin pasta.

Pre-heat the oven to 190°C. Lightly coat the courgettes, carrots and asparagus in the oil and place in the oven for 10-15 minutes. Combine the tomatoes and herbs, mix together with a splash of oil and leave to one side.

For the tonno, cook the rabbit meat in barely simmering water for 2 hours with a bay leaf. Drain the meat and sprinkle with oil. Pre-heat the oven to 55°C.

Ensure that all the bones have been removed from the fish, then coat in extra virgin olive oil and cook in the oven for 1 hour.

Cook the pasta in plenty of boiling salted water to your liking, and sauté together with the cooked vegetables, tomatoes, meat and fish until everything is heated through. In another pan sauté the breadcrumbs with a splash of olive oil, the garlic, salt and parsley and sprinkle over the pasta, then serve.

Wine suggestion: White – Derthona, Vigneti Massa (Timorasso)

"Pecora nell'Orto"
"Sheep in the Veg Garden"

Michele explains that the whole point of this recipe is that it's seasonal so choose whatever vegetables are particularly good at the time. He uses 18-month to 2-year old Gigante Bergamasco lamb meat, but any lamb or hogget loin will do.

200g mixed seasonal vegetables per person, such as fennel, courgettes, asparagus, carrots, peas, green beans, radishes, cauliflower

Extra virgin olive oil

Herbs, whatever you like with the vegetables you're using

Garlic, finely chopped, to taste,

Salt and pepper

100g lamb or hogget loin per person, thinly sliced

Pre-heat the oven to 180°C.

Cut the vegetables into small pieces and mix with a little olive oil, the chopped herbs, garlic, salt and pepper. Roast in the oven until they're cooked, but still crunchy.

Shortly before the vegetables are done, cook the meat briefly on a hot plate or griddle pan, turning over so that the slices are cooked on both sides. Combine the meat and vegetables and serve immediately.

Wine suggestion: Red – Ronchi di Brescia IGT, Cà del Vént (Cabernet Sauvignon, Merlot, Nebbiolo)

Da Vittorio
Enrico "Chicco" and Roberto "Bobo" Cerea

via Cantalupa, 17
24060 Brusaporto
T: +39 035 681 024
W: davittoro.com

Opening hours: 12.00 –
14.30; 19.30 – 22.30
Closed: Wed lunch
Holidays: 20 days in Aug

Driving up to the Da Vittorio villa through its lushly verdant grounds emphasises the feeling that you're moving from real life to a world apart. From passing through a nondescript residential zone you're now entering a place where everything is gleaming and sumptuous but relaxed and friendly.

But behind the elegance of the mid-morning scene, the staff are anything but carefree. There's a professional determination to get things done: iron table linens, check that glasses are spotless and that cutlery is precisely aligned. However, this isn't preparation for an extraordinary banquet but a regular lunchtime service in a restaurant. Albeit one with three Michelin stars.

Enrico and Roberto Cerea are brothers who became chefs, took over their parents' restaurant (the name comes from their father who set it up originally with his wife Bruna in central Bergamo), and took it to the highest level of haute cuisine. Chicco and Bobo (as they are known) are now the most visible faces of Da Vittorio, but there's an enterprising family and a large team behind them that they generously acknowledge.

The brothers are matter-of-fact but moved when talking about their parents; how they suffered in the Second World War and how they dreamt of opening a restaurant. It was the fulfilment of that dream that sowed the seed of today's quite extraordinary Da Vittorio organisation.

Fast-forward five decades and for all the plaudits, worldwide acclaim, and renown of the front guys, it's still a very grounded business. Even Bruna continues to help out. She may now be a doting and graceful grandmother but her work ethic — and that of her children — is mind-blowing.

Aside from Chicco and Bobo in the kitchen, there's also the accomplished

Paolo Rota, their brother-in-law. Paolo is a quietly commanding talent, but one who works his oven gloves off and organises a team of enthusiastic and eager-to-impress youngsters while dissolving silently into the background when it's time for praise.

It's not just about organising staff, of course; there's also the ongoing need to develop new recipes and stay on top of the culinary game. Chicco believes his inquisitiveness is a big help to his creativity in the kitchen. "I'm curious like a child and always want to try new things," he says. But this isn't random play. There's a genuine interest in what other countries and cuisines are doing. "I think that the trends and movements in Spain are incredibly important," he explains. "They've helped stimulate our imagination. As has Scandinavia with its affable service and friendly explanations to diners. I like these approaches." Bobo's keen to embrace new things too and even at his high level would still look at doing a *stage* somewhere. "I'm always up for that. You have to keep learning."

Despite their involvement in recipe development, both Chicco and Bobo would love to spend more regular time in the kitchen. "I love being at the stove, and that buzz of the frontline," says Bobo. Chicco refuses to say which of the dishes he's created is his favourite. "If I name one I'll be doing wrong by the others. It would be like choosing one of my children." But however important the appearance of a plate of food is here, Bobo explains that "the starting point with every recipe we develop is the taste. Of course we use the best produce we can get, we may embellish it beautifully with a foam or something novel, but it all starts with the taste." Just as Cole

Above right: Bruna, Rossella and Gigi the dog

Opposite top: Paolo Rota

Porter's lyrics are wonderful with music but still masterful without it, you can't help feeling that the Cerea brothers' food will always impress, even without the flourishes.

On its own their development of a three-starred restaurant in Brusaporto would be impressive. But the brothers also run, among other enterprises, a one-starred restaurant in St. Moritz (open only during the ski season) and a catering company that takes transportable fine feasting to new levels.

But simply prepared food hasn't been forgotten. After all, Chicco's memory retains the joys of "polenta with slow-cooked *guanciale* or even warm bread with fresh mortadella". Those joys are evident in their bistro at Bergamo airport "with no lobster, caviar or foie gras, just good, simple food," as Chicco puts it. "Italian simplicity is *buonissima* and people who come to Italy want to eat good pasta, *tagliata di manzo* and a good tiramisù, so we serve quickly made plates of food, but using excellent raw ingredients." Chicco is sure that their *cavallo di battaglia* (literally 'war horse' but an English speaker would probably say 'trump card') is "our *tagliatelle al ragù* with house-made pasta, cooked to order, mixed with butter and served with a four-hour beef ragù and freshly grated Parmesan." Not bad for a quick bite pre-boarding. But then Chicco passes by the airport on his way to work so pops in on most days to "check the sauces. It's important to keep an eye on things," he says.

Not everybody who flies into Bergamo and wants to eat Cerea brothers' creations does so at the airport, of course. There are lots of international 'regulars' who make the trip to Da Vittorio whenever they can. The great and the good of Europe obviously come along, but so too does Middle Eastern royalty. And there's one visitor — from Brazil — who flies in twice a year for three or four days.

So it's an advantage that there are rooms at Da Vittorio. Rossella (one of the Cerea sisters) looks after the stunning Relais & Chateaux accommodation above the restaurant. Which means you can ease gently from a fabulous meal and perhaps take a stroll around the grounds before retiring. And then wake up to a feast of a breakfast. But as Bobo says, "When somebody comes here we want them to leave their problems behind."

Rossella was also responsible for the unrestrained bonbon trolley and leads decisions on the design aesthetic and furniture. The main dining room was carefully organised so there's no 'Siberia' (that is, second-class seating). It's light and airy in contrast to the snug and cosy bar run by Francesco,

another brother who is responsible too for the renowned wine cellar.

There are also numerous events held that, at first glance, appear to be more fun than fine dining. For instance a pizza and fizz evening (Chicco loves bubbly; the house fizz is Ca' del Bosco). In keeping with the diligent approach, the brothers had people from Naples come along to help with a Neapolitan buffet including six different pizzas and top-of-the-range Champagne and Franciacorta.

Which is indicative of the entertaining — and at times theatrical — element to eating at Da Vittorio. Take one of the restaurant's signature dishes, a pasta dish which couldn't — theoretically — be simpler: Paccheri with a Tomato and Grana Padano Sauce. Except it's an example of Da Vittorio's scrupulous attention to detail. Bobo explains, "In simplicity it's easy to make mistakes: to get the temperature or quantities wrong or to grate the cheese incorrectly. And the tomatoes have to be specific types. Because it's not done by accident." And it's also flamboyantly served from a trolley by whichever chef is available. Although, according to Bobo, "Chicco's the one with the talent for the 'show cooking.'"

But Bobo is keen on *primi* and so it's unsurprising that there's a pasta dish which is elevated to such a high spot. As he summarises, "I think that in Italian cooking, the *primi piatti* are the most important because in other cuisines around the world you have an entrée and a main course but the *primo piatto* is Italian."

Everyone in the family comments on how tiring and demanding the work is but neither Chicco or Bobo can imagine doing anything else. Bobo laments the number of youngsters who see edited glimpses of the restaurant world on competitive TV cooking programmes and only realise how difficult and relentless it is when they sign up and start dealing with the practicalities. You can have a comfortable glimpse of this by eating here: as a diner you get a great view into the kitchen through a large glass window. Professional kitchen theatre without the exhaustion.

But as arduous as working life is (and 'complacency' isn't a word that features in the Cerea family vocabulary), with this number of projects, nobody has much spare time, although Bobo is a keen sailor and his annual boating holiday is eagerly anticipated. For a few years, Chicco has been learning to play golf. Typically, however, despairing of the refreshments served, he created an organisation called RistoGolf, which takes sustenance on the links to new levels. "Every two or three holes we stop to eat," he explains. "We make something there and then, perhaps fry something simple. Some golfers like to stop for a *tramezzino* but I prefer to organise some Champagne and some simple cooking." By 'simple' he means toqued chefs along the fairway.

Back in the beautiful villa of Da Vittorio, half an hour before the restaurant opens for lunch, a couple arrive without a reservation. Well, but very casually heeled for an upmarket restaurant they ask if they can be served quickly because they have a long drive to France ahead. The receptionist checks with the kitchen and they're seen through to the dining room immediately. That's the kind of service you get at Da Vittorio.

Before Chicco returns to the kitchen, he talks about people becoming obsessed with gaining Michelin stars and the ensuing frustration. "Just do what you do well. You have to do what you're happiest doing and what you do best." And it helps to have a talented, very hard working and extraordinarily energetic team around you.

Fun and friendly may not be the first words that spring to mind when thinking about most three-star establishments but Da Vittorio is different. It artfully weaves together the highest luxury with the charm of a feelgood family restaurant.

Uova di Quaglia in Cocotte, Pomodoro, Burrata e Verdure Verdi
Quail's Egg en Cocotte, Tomato, Burrata and Green Vegetables

At Da Vittorio the green tomato mousse is served in a tomato shaped sugar case, which is challenging to do at home. Cooking the quail's eggs in the pea cream is fiddly but rather fun once you get the hang of it. This dish should really be appreciated at the restaurant, but a reasonable attempt of assembling the flavours and colours can be made at home, with some simplifications.

SERVES 4

Tomato mousse:

400g of green tomatoes

A few basil leaves

5g gelatine

60ml extra virgin olive oil

Pea cream:

½ onion, chopped

1 tbsp spoon olive oil

300g peas, parboiled

50ml fresh double cream

10 mint leaves

50ml vegetable stock

A few chard leaves

Bay leaf

8 quail's eggs

500g burrata

3 green tomatoes, sliced

Olive oil

Pepper

Handful of fresh broad beans

A few asparagus spears, parboiled

Knob of butter

Vegetable stock, reduced

Grating of liquorice

To make the mousse, put the tomatoes and basil in a blender and blitz until you have a thick mixture. Add the hydrated gelatine, as per packet instructions, and the oil. Mix together and keep in the fridge until set.

To make the pea cream, soften the onion in a pan with the oil. Add the peas, cream, mint and stock. Bring to the boil and leave until the peas are cooked. Adjust the seasoning and put everything in a blender. Blitz thoroughly and then press through a fine sieve so that you have a creamy mixture.

Next, cook the chard in boiling water with the bay. Drain and discard the bay leaf. Season the burrata and the sliced tomatoes with oil and pepper.

To cook the quail's eggs, take a square of cling film and place a large teaspoon of pea cream in the centre and spread it out to form a circle. Break

a quail's egg into the middle of this and close up the cling film so that the egg is surrounded by pea cream. Tie a firm knot so that the parcels are securely closed. Suspend these parcels in boiling water for 3 minutes. Remove with kitchen tweezers, and leave for a minute. Alternatively, to make it easier, just softly boil the eggs and shell them before adding to the finished dish.

While you are preparing the eggs, warm up the remaining pea cream, the broad beans and the asparagus with a knob of butter.

To serve, start by putting a base of warmed pea cream on each plate, then lay the vegetables, the eggs, the burrata and a spoon of tomato mousse on top of this. Cut and remove the cling film from the eggs with pea cream and place onto each plate.

Season everything with reduced vegetable stock and a grating of liquorice to taste.

Wine suggestion: White – Curtefranco Bianco, Cà del Bosco (Chardonnay, Pinot Bianco) or Calvarino Soave Classico Superiore, Pieropan (Garganega, Trebbiano di Soave)

Piccione con Pomodori Canditi e Olive Taggiasche, Insalatina di Campo
Pigeon with Candied Tomatoes and Taggiasche Olives, Small Field Salad

At Da Vittorio they sous vide the pigeon breasts and legs which is not the easiest option for the home cook. This recipe has been radically adapted for domestic kitchens as it's difficult to replicate their version. But even without their skill and flair, it's still an impressive plate of food. Note that you may need to adjust certain quantities if your pigeons are on the small side.

SERVES 4

8 pigeon breasts

8 pigeon legs

200ml meat stock

40g Taggiasche olive tapenade

1 heaped tsp chopped fresh oregano

Zest from half an unwaxed lemon

8 candied or sun dried tomato halves

1 large potato, peeled

1 tbsp mascarpone

200g cooked polenta, cut into small triangles

1 tbsp grated Parmesan

100g butter

Tempura batter (made by mixing approx. 20g flour with a pinch of bicarbonate of soda, 1 tsp cornflour and 30ml chilled sparkling water)

100g small salad leaves

Extra virgin olive oil

Bring a pan of water up to 60°C and poach the pigeon breasts for 15 minutes, trying to maintain a steady temperature throughout. Braise the legs in a pan of meat stock for about 5 minutes. Drain and leave to one side.

Remove the breasts from the water and drain on kitchen towel. Cut a large slit in them and stuff each with a smear of tapenade, a sprinkle of fresh oregano, some lemon zest and a tomato half.

Use a mandolin to slice the potato lengthwise into 16 thin slices. Before the slices have time to dry out, or discolour, place a small amount of tapenade in the centre of half the slices and then cover each one with the remaining potato slices. Removing any air, press the edges closed to form potato ravioli.

Spread the mascarpone on to the polenta and sprinkle with Parmesan.

Heat the butter in a pan and brown the pigeon breasts. Fry the potato ravioli until the potato is cooked and becoming golden at the edges. Keep them warm.

Coat the legs in tempura batter and fry in plenty of sesame seed oil. Briefly grill the polenta triangles so that the cheese melts and becomes lightly brown.

Dress the salad leaves lightly with olive oil and then arrange all the components on a plate. Spoon on any cooking juices and serve.

Wine suggestion: Red – Carmenero Rosso, Cà del Bosco (Carmenère) or San Lorenzo Valtellina Superiore Sassella, Mamete Prevostini (Nebbiolo)

Busto Arsizio

On the outskirts of Milan, between the city centre and Malpensa airport, is the town of Busto Arsizio. Although it fails to make many tourist itineraries, it has a likeable, unpretentious feel about it.

It also has the most important baroque church in the province of Varese. The Basilica di San Giovanni Battista is in the centre of town, near to some interesting independent shops and bakeries, all with helpful staff.

Osteria La Rava e la Fava
Fabio Rivolta

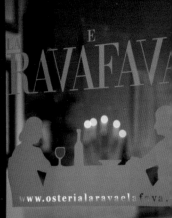

via Milano, 4
21052 Busto Arsizio
T: +39 0331 320 340 /
+39 366 150 3135
W: osterialaravaelafava.it

Opening hours: 12.00 –
14.30; 19.30 – 23.00
Closed: Wed
Holidays: 10 days in Jan and
20 days in Aug

La Rava e la Fava established its reputation in the Varese town of Busto Arsizio. Its original location — a corner on an industrial estate — wasn't exciting but the food was excellent, and it was the perfect place for lunch when flying into or out of Malpensa airport.

In some ways version two couldn't be more different. Since November 2014 La Rava e la Fava has occupied a place in a little independent retail hub. In a pedestrianised area at the end of an oleander-filled courtyard next to the Basilica di San Giovanni Battista in what used to be a cinema, there's a neighbouring and community-minded historic bookshop too.

Originally the idea was to use the tables in front of the bar at the entrance for lunch and the back of the room for dinner but on the first day 80 workers turned up for their midday break. Soon it was either open up the back of the room at lunchtime or turn away 50 covers every day.

The main rush starts, predictably, just after one o'clock. Despite the impressive number of lunchtime diners, it's a relaxing place; the music is at just the right volume and there's the soft murmur of people chatting and taking a breather. The osteria also offers a great value menu. For little more than the price of a processed, over-chilled take-away 'meal' in some parts of the world, you can enjoy a couple of plates of freshly cooked seasonal food.

Fabio kept the name when he moved — and why not? He'd spent 12 years building up a following and it's a great — and very evocative — name. It comes from the expression '*raccontare la rava e la fava.*' Based on farmers' jargon (referring to turnips and broad beans), it means to tell the whole story from start to finish. "It's a local saying," he explains, "and reflects our philosophy. You can enter, sit down, drink and chat and we won't ask you to move on. You can take your time here."

At lunchtime and in the morning people are usually too busy to linger, however. At the end of the day it's a different matter, especially on evenings when there are performances on the small stage at the back of the dining room — perhaps a blues band, or a group singing in Milanese dialect.

Fabio was born in Busto Arsizio and although his father wasn't involved in food or wine professionally, he was irrepressibly enthusiastic about both, and that enthusiasm was passed on to his son — so much so that Fabio went to catering school.

A few years later, when he was working at a traditional Milanese restaurant on the Navigli, he started thinking about setting up a small traditional osteria of his own, and (this being Italy) serious consideration was given to serving foods from the *territorio*. However, Busto Arsizio "doesn't have many culinary traditions. It's always been a working town," as Fabio puts it. Dishes typically involved cheap cuts of meat that could be put in the oven in the morning before work, cooked slowly, and be ready by the evening.

Nevertheless, and even though the area surrounding Busto Arsizio isn't agricultural, Fabio has done all he can to use as much local produce as possible, starting with fruit and vegetables from small nearby growers. And over the years he's added Slow Food presidia to the menu: *prosciutto di maiale grigio del Casentino*, *violino di capra* from the Valchiavenna and Bitto Storico cheese and what he describes as 'fantastic *cotechini*' from his *salumi* maker in Mantua.

And there's food on sale that Fabio rates highly: biscuits, oils, beans and cured meats, all displayed alongside lots of dramatically large artworks and a big telephone sign in front of the loos — a memento from the original osteria.

There are also numerous smaller ornaments behind the bar from Barcelona, Goa and Mumbai. They are meant to bring good luck. However, as the osteria of choice for the locals from the word go, La Rava e la Fava probably doesn't need much of that.

Top left: the entrance to the osteria, through the courtyard of independent shops

Top right: lunchtime at the osteria

Bottom: Fabio Rivolta

Penne La Rava e La Fava
La Rava e La Fava's Penne

It's only appropriate that a restaurant with 'fava', broad bean, in its name should have a popular dish including them on its menu. This is as easy and as quick as it gets for home cooking.

SERVES 4

320g ridged penne

Extra virgin olive oil

2 Ramato tomatoes, diced

**2 large handfuls of fresh, double-
    podded broad beans**

Salt and pepper

8 basil leaves, torn roughly by hand

Cook the penne in plenty of salted water. While they're cooking, put the oil into a cold pan and on to the heat. When the oil starts to sizzle add the tomatoes, the broad beans, salt and pepper.

Leave to cook for a few minutes and then pour in a drop of pasta water and leave to simmer briefly so it starts to be absorbed.

When the pasta is al dente, drain and place in the pan with the tomatoes and broad beans then remove from the heat. Add the basil and a drizzle of olive oil. Mix everything well and serve while hot.

Wine suggestion: White – a Müller-Thurgau from the Alto Adige

Bruscitti
Bruscitti

This is a classic dish from Busto Arsizio; bruscitti means 'crumbs' in reference to the small pieces of beef although there are different spellings. Originally made with cheap cuts, today most recipes specify something more expensive.

Lardo can be used instead of pancetta, but then reduce the amount of butter accordingly. Erbabono (which used to be foraged for in hedges) was listed in the original recipe and is now replaced by fennel seeds. The meat isn't browned as it's believed that the crust impedes the "perfect mixture of butter and meat juice." Originally, the pan was placed in the embers of the fireplace as people left to work in the fields, and without further stirring or attention, this would be ready when they returned.

SERVES 6

1.8kg beef, a mix of brisket and cheeks

90g butter (and more if needed)

90g unsmoked pancetta, chopped

Salt and pepper

A bouquet garni, including a heaped tsp of fennel seeds, and (optionally) a small clove of garlic

175ml robust red wine

Polenta, to serve

With a sharp knife, cut the meat into almond sized pieces. Put into a large cold pan with the butter, pancetta, salt and a scant amount of pepper, and the bouquet garni. Cover and cook over a very low heat for 2-3 hours, until the meat is done. Some people cover the meat with a *cartouche* (a disc of waxed paper) to ensure the steam doesn't escape. It's advisable to check and stir occasionally with a wooden spoon. If it's too dry, only add butter, not stock, but if it's too wet, remove the cover for a while so that it dries out. Depending on how low your heat is, and the amount of fat in your meats, you may well have to add an additional quantity of butter.

When the meat is cooked, remove the bouquet garni, add the wine and increase the heat for a few minutes. Reduce the heat again until "the initial harsh smell of the wine has passed." Serve immediately with freshly cooked polenta.

Wine suggestion: Red – Ghemme Monsecco, Zanetta Sergio E Valter (Nebbiolo)

Cernobbio

Cernobbio is an attractive town on the western side of Lake Como. It's well known for being home to the deluxe hotel of Villa d'Este. For those with less extravagant budgets, there are benches beneath the trees near to the ferry stop where visitors can sit and take in the view, or have a drink at a bar on the lakeside square.

You might also choose to take a short promenade along the waterfront. However, for the more energetic, the start of the 125 km hike along La Via dei Monti Lariani (which ends in Sorico at the northern most point of the lake) starts here.

Trattoria del Glicine
Mario Pozzi

via Vittorio Veneto, 1
Piazza S. Stefano
22012 Cernobbio
T: +39 031 511 332

Opening hours: 12.30 –
14.00; 19.30 – 22.30
Closed: Mon evening
and Tues
Holidays: 30 Dec – 6 Jan

It's an uphill walk from the predictably well-appointed landing stage at Lake
Como's Cernobbio to Trattoria del Glicine. But 15 minutes of gentle
exertion is not such a bad idea if you want to work up an appetite, or at
least kid yourself that you've earned a serious lunch. Or even if you just
want to move away from the tourist magnets on the waterfront.

Glicine means wisteria, which is fitting as the outside terrace of this trattoria
is covered by a magnificent one that's over 100 years old. When Mario
Pozzi, the trattoria's chef owner who was born and bred just down the road,
acquired and redecorated the premises, the wisteria was the only thing he
didn't change. He felt it was too well established (he can still remember
seeing it as a child) and certainly too beautiful to remove. And of course, he
paid tribute to it when he named the trattoria.

In the younger days of the wisteria, back in the early 1900s, the building at
1 Via Vittorio Veneto, a few feet from the cemetery, belonged to a local
cooperative. It later became an, allegedly, unremarkable pizzeria. But it was
always a social meeting place for the locals, not least of all because back in
the 1950s it housed the only TV in the village. That made it quite a draw. It
was also where the nearby elders came in the afternoon for a coffee and
glass of wine while settling down to play cards until dinner time. Mario kept
that welcome going when he took over, although after about a year and a
half most of the ageing card players had "moved next door," as he delicately
puts it.

Mario was always determined to create an ambience in keeping with the
surroundings and beauty of the old building. As he says, "It's not often that
you find old buildings with rooms this big. These are the sorts of spaces
you'd find in very upmarket houses."

And he is nothing if not visually aware, having worked successfully for many years in the textile business. It's been an important Como industry for centuries, and one in which his adored grandmother was a trailblazer. And then some: she ran her own department in a textiles dyeing plant back in the early 1900s. She was always known, says Mario, "as Maria 'Capa' or 'boss'. Everyone, even those who'd never worked for her, called her that, so people believed it was her proper name."

Mario was well regarded too. Clients would arrive with design ideas and he would work with them to produce beautiful fabrics. But after nearly three decades of this, he needed a change. He spent a couple of years "looking for my own path," and in the meantime, as he'd always done, he'd cook dinner at home for friends. Not for a mere five or six, but often as many as 40. Repeatedly, people would say to him, "This is what you should be doing; this is your path." So finally, he decided to take his first steps.

And his years of looking after clients in the textile industry have stood him in good stead. He's still very client-focused, and on a busy evening service, talks to every table, without once over-staying his welcome.

You can tell it's not a tourist place, not just because there are lots of locals eating here, but because there is some well researched and carefully chosen international food on the menu. As a visitor you may not be interested in eating Texan beef, but Mario wants to give his regulars variety and is keen to stress to Italians that Italy isn't the only place with great food.

Above left: Mario Pozzi

Above right: the wisteria on the terrace

And he welcomes foreigners to his trattoria. As he's well aware, they tend to be people who are well travelled and keen to get off the most obvious routes. But then that's the sort of curious traveller he is too, loving to set off in his camper van to go exploring. Perhaps to Germany, Budapest or Picardy where "every so often we stop to drink a glass of wine and sample something from the *territorio* that we don't know."

But back at home, he still gets excited about produce and — he's a qualified sommelier — champions the wine as well as the food of Lombardy. On one occasion he held an evening with a focus on the Valtellina and its wines. Rather than just serve *pizzoccheri*, the traditional Valtellina pasta, he took the ingredients of Bitto, cabbage and potatoes and wrapped them in ravioli-like parcels to create a '*raviocchero*', or a ravioli *pizzocchero*. They were a real hit throughout that winter, apparently.

Beppe, who is a chef but also a loyal customer, comes from Como when his schedule permits. "I love the way he's so engaged and can explain to everyone all aspects of what he cooks," Beppe says. "Sometimes I ask him in advance, to cook special things for me. Last week he prepared a whole meal of snails – antipasto, primo and secondo. That's the way to treat your regulars," he beams.

On a hot summer's day, it all feels calming and comfortable up at Trattoria del Glicine, with the sun dappling through the wisteria on to the terrace outside. Catching glimpses of the lake after a fine lunch it's a relief to know that the walk back is downhill.

Insalata Tiepida di Baccalà
Warm Salt Cod Salad

You need the best quality salt cod for this. Soak it according to the instructions by covering with cold water and changing it several times. Depending on its thickness and dryness, this could take from 24 – 72 hours to rehydrate. Taste periodically, it should still be salty but not overpoweringly so. Otherwise, even though it won't have the same depth of flavour, substitute fresh cod, salted for a day.

INGREDIENTS PER PERSON:

120g salt cod, cleaned and soaked

8 Pachino cherry tomatoes, halved

4 tbsp extra virgin olive oil

**1 tbsp finely chopped basil and
   parsley**

Remove any skin and bones from the soaked salt cod.

In a pan, heat the tomatoes in the oil for just 1 minute, then add the chopped herbs. Steam the salt cod briefly (Mario does his for 30 seconds), until heated through and cooked to your preference. Place the fish and tomatoes on a plate and dress with the oil and herbs from the pan.

Wine suggestion: White – Chardonnay Langhe DOC, Tenute Cisa Asinari dei Marchesi di Gresy (Chardonnay)

Lavarello in Carpione
Lake Fish in Carpione

Lavarello is a freshwater fish found in Lake Como. This method of preparing fresh fish enables it to be kept for a few days and is a popular Lombard antipasto.

SERVES 4

Marinade:

4 white onions, thinly sliced

2 celery sticks, thinly sliced

4 basil leaves

4 sage leaves

4 sprigs of thyme

4 sprigs of parsley

500ml white wine

250ml red wine vinegar

Salt and pepper

Fish:

8 white fish fillets, approx. 150g each

Flour

Nut oil

Salt

To make the marinade, put all the marinade ingredients into a saucepan. Bring to the boil and leave on a gentle heat for 30-40 minutes until the onions are soft. Taste and season.

Coat the fish fillets lightly in flour and fry them in nut oil. Drain them on kitchen towel, and lightly salt them. Place them in a dish and cover them with the warm marinade. Once cool, cover and leave to marinate in the fridge for 24 hours. These should keep in the fridge for approximately 4-5 days.

Serve at room temperature.

Wine suggestion: White – "La Moglie del Re", Cantina Angelinetta, Lago di

Cremona

Cremona is famous for violins (it's where Antonio Stradivari was born and worked). There are statues, enthralling shop displays, a museum and a concert hall. As if that wasn't musical enough, the Baroque composer Monteverdi hails from here too.

At Christmas time the town lights beautifully enhance their surroundings: a tall tower with a cascade of simple white lights falling to earth, or a partially hidden square illuminated by a single decorated tree.

The town's food specialities include *mostarda di Cremona* and *torrone*: the Sperlari shop with its old-style packaging is the place to head for

Hosteria 700
Natalina Fenocchio and Marina Morelli

Piazza Gallina, 1
26100 Cremona
T: +39 037 236 175
W: hosteria700.it

Opening hours: 12.30 –
14.30; 19.30 – 22.00
Closed: Mon evening
and Tues
Holidays: variable

The inside of Hosteria 700 in the centre of Cremona couldn't be more of a surprise. Behind an unassuming door and entrance is an old palazzo. Given the very high, decorated ceilings, a chandelier and a wine list that includes Ornellaia and some of the best Franciacorta names, you're probably thinking fine dining with prices to match. Think again.

Friends Marina and Lina, who run Hosteria 700, cook and serve mostly traditional Cremonese food in a setting of comfortable, worn opulence, a setting that makes it easy to feel relaxed.

But that isn't just down to the faded grandeur. Both women have enough expertise to look calm and serene even when working flat out.

They've known each other a long time and are a strong team. Each has an understanding and respect for what the other does because, although Marina's domain is the kitchen and Lina's is front of house, they frequently, albeit briefly, move around when needed, Marina serving a table and greeting people, and Lina helping out with making pasta and desserts.

The menu features pasta filled with pumpkin and served with butter and thyme as well as *tortelli* of aubergines, black olives and tomatoes named after Monteverdi, a reminder, if one were needed, of where we are. And every second Thursday of the month is risotto night. Alongside their house risotto, with rocket, speck and scamorza, you'll also find more unusual combinations such as liquorice and saffron.

On a bright summer's day, the sun floods in through the large windows and all feels well with the world. Being Cremona, there's likely to be lots of artistic types, whether at lunchtime or in the evening. In fact a famous

singer once told Lina, "You're a virtuoso." Given the standard of artistic brilliance in town, that's quite a compliment.

Both women stress how important it is that people feel at ease and at home when dining with them. And that, along with classic food in civilised surroundings, is what Hosteria 700 offers you. Even if it's only the home of your dreams

Salumi con Mostarda dell'Hosteria 700
Salumi with Hosteria 700 Mostarda

Mostarda di Cremona or mustard fruit is a sweet and hot condiment. Mustard essence is very difficult to get hold of in the UK (buy it from a pharmacy when in Italy), and is very, very strong. Use it with a lot of care and keep it well out of the way of babies, young children and pets etc. At Hosteria 700, they serve their home made mostarda with a selection of salumi such as coppa, pancetta or spalla cotta.

9 x 200g sterilised preserving jars

500g pears, Williams are good

500g green apples

500g lemons

500g oranges

1kg white caster sugar

15 drops of mustard essence

Wash the fruit well, remove the cores and pips and cut into smallish pieces. Put into a bowl, add the sugar, cover and leave in a cool place for 24 hours.

Transfer to a large saucepan, bring quickly to the boil and simmer while partially covered for 15 minutes. Leave in the pan for 24 hours. Repeat for another 5 days, i.e. simmer gently for 15 minutes then leave for 24 hours. Towards the end take care that it doesn't catch, and if it is too runny, leave uncovered so that it reduces. You should end up with a thick mixture.

Very carefully add the drops of mustard essence and mix thoroughly. Put into the jars and store in the fridge and serve alongside boiled meats and salumi.

Wine suggestion: Red – Bonarda or Franciacorta – Bellavista Alma Cuvée Brut (Chardonnay, Pinot Nero, Pinot Bianco)

Marubini Cremonesi in Brodo
Cremona's Marubini in a Meat Broth

These pretty filled pasta parcels are a speciality of Cremona.

SERVES 4

Filling:

300g meat (a mix of whatever cheap cuts you have such as beef, chicken and veal)

1 small onion, peeled and halved

1 small carrot, peeled and halved

1 celery stick, halved

125g soft salami, or cooked sausage meat filling

1 egg

Small handful of grated Parmesan

Salt, to taste

Pasta:

500g 00 flour

5 eggs

Drop of olive oil

Put the 300g of meat and the vegetables in a pan. Add water to cover by about 4cm. Cover and cook for 3 – 3.5 hours on a low heat ensuring the pan doesn't dry out.

Make the pasta dough, cover and leave to rest.

Remove the meat taking care to keep the cooking liquid. Mince the cooked meats. Add the sausage meat, egg, cheese and salt. Mix well.

Roll the pasta out thinly and cut into approx. 5-6 cm squares. Add a scant teaspoon of filling, fold over to form a triangle, wrap this around your finger and press it closed.

Cook the parcels for 10 minutes in the heated meat broth and serve the pasta parcels in the broth.

Wine suggestion: Red – Gutturnio (Barbera, Croatina) or Lambrusco Frizzante

Antica Trattoria del Gallo
Paolo Reina

via Privata Gerli, 1
Vigano Certosino
20083 Gaggiano
T: +39 02 908 5276
W: trattoriadelgallo.com

Opening hours: 12.30-14.00;
19.30-22.00
Closed: Mon and Tues
Holidays: 24 Dec – 5 Jan
and 10-20 Aug

"Us too!" clamoured Paolo Reina and one of his two inseparable friends. The third member of their group had just told the school that he wanted to go to catering college. The other two had no idea what they wanted to do next, but they knew the three of them had to stick together.

It's one of the more unusual reasons for entering a professional kitchen but it's not the only moment of serendipity in Paolo's working life. For example, he now owns one of the oldest trattorie in Italy, a mere 3km from where he was brought up. He first worked there in the mid '80s. But he shouldn't have been anywhere near home; he was supposed to be refining his skills in the USA. "I came back from doing a season in Switzerland and was about to go to LA," he explains. "My mother was very much against that idea as she thought she'd never see me again."

So instead of the bright lights of the Hollywood Hills, maternal pressure took him to the nearby kitchen of Antica Trattoria del Gallo, where he was told on his arrival to leave his prized chef's knives to one side and use an old yellow handled blade. Chopping veg for hours, in a trattoria that pretty much only served chicken (*gallo* means rooster), was not the next step he'd hoped for.

But he's a positive and hard-working sort, and he impressed the trattoria's owners, the Gerli family, with his attitude — so much so in fact that even though he moved on in less than a year, he was later called up with an offer by the matriarch of the family. She felt it was time for the Gerlis to call it a day and asked if he wanted to take over.

It was an exciting offer, but also a challenging one; he'd never managed a restaurant before, let alone one that had been around since 1870. But he had

Above centre: Paolo Reina

run kitchens and after much deliberating, decided to go for it as long as the Signora agreed to work alongside him for six months. This she did. But then she died, leaving Paolo in charge on his own with serious debts.

He also had a regular clientele who knew what they were going to order before they arrived — which was not quite as serious a problem as the debt, but still a challenge. He explains, "People came here and they ate what was on offer. Which was the chicken. There was one waiter who would never admit that there was only one *secondo*. If someone said "I don't really like chicken. What else do you have?" he'd reply, "Well, we have steak but it's really not very good. You're better off with the chicken"."

Things have changed considerably — and wonderfully — in the intervening quarter of a century. The staff are helpful, professional, fun and knowledgeable about the much broader menu. Chicken is still there but Paolo has introduced all manner of other things that he loves: *cotechino* with lentils, *ravioli di vitello al burro versato* and creative desserts.

Interestingly for an Italian cook, the food served at home was not the stuff of maternal legend, "I never understood how my mother managed to make such an inedible minestrone," says Paolo. His father loved fishing and would go out to the water at three in the morning before work, coming back with quite a catch. It all went to friends as Paolo's mother "didn't cook fish".

These days, Paolo serves both lake fish and *baccalà* in his trattoria as well as anchovies, which neatly sum up his view on superb raw ingredients: "If you have a perfect anchovy there's nothing more you can add to it."

If the name didn't hint at the restaurant's former reputation, the huge number of rooster and chicken ornaments around the place surely would. All of them are presents from friends and guests. Only a fraction of the collection is on display at any one time though; most of the 1,000 are waiting in the wings, so to speak.

Unlike the real chickens and the strutting rooster in Paolo's *orto*. They love to take centre stage and have a glorious existence, but then Paolo takes great care of everything in his *orto*. He may not be able to produce everything there that the restaurant needs, but tending the fruit and veg keeps him in touch with how things grow, and going along to weed, pick and collect eggs provides a rare moment of calm.

Paolo is respectful of tradition but not unthinkingly slavish to it. He sees himself as only a small part of the trattoria's history so some things are not for changing. Especially not *the* chicken dish, which predates Paolo and is still on the menu. It's called *Pollo alla Diavola*, even though it isn't actually *Pollo alla Diavola* at all. "But it's always had the wrong name. We can't change that now."

But he did change the trattoria a few years back, redecorating it so that it's now a bright, colourful place. There are photos of food to link the dining room with the kitchen. "We hang photographs that people can buy and we're forever changing the tablecloths and the flowers so that if you come here frequently you don't get tired of it all," he says. "The menu changes every 30 days. It's like a marriage; you don't want people to get bored."

Antica Trattoria del Gallo is on the edge of an unexciting suburb, but Milan is only minutes away and many of the restaurant's loyal and enthusiastic customers make the trip from the big city. It's very popular with families and big groups at the weekend, especially when they're given the chance to sit outside on the covered terrace. And before they leave perhaps they'll buy favourite foods to take home.

"The *bottega* at the entrance was a dream of mine," says Paolo. "You can buy what you've eaten here — say capers or hazelnuts. We even produce things, like *biscotti*, that you can take away. If you have a sick grandmother at home then you can take her a piece of cake."

Or perhaps some salami for yourself. Paolo spent three years working with a salami maker. They removed everything they considered superfluous. "Years ago, pepper and garlic were added because there were no fridges," Paolo says. "Our salami contains only pork, salt, and one glass of wine per 100kg

of meat. You'd never eat a whole grain of pepper so why put them in salami? If you want pepper on your salami, then add good freshly milled pepper once you've sliced it."

He also bakes bread every day but that's for selfish reasons, "I just love the aroma," he says. And let's not start on the glorious smell of the wonderful cheese trolley (though you should steer clear if mould upsets you). "We're near to Milan so we can't source everything right here, but we have great longstanding producers and lots of *cascine* nearby."

And it's those relationships with producers and friends, both chefs and patrons who are running places with the same ideals, that help to keep him happy, curious and driven. In fact you can't imagine Paolo being happier doing anything else. Thank goodness one of his teenage mates wanted to be a chef.

Frittata alle Erbe di Campo con Robiola e Pomodoro Fresco
Wild Herb Frittata with Robiola and Fresh Tomato Sauce

Paolo only makes this in spring, when herbs are new and fresh. He advises breaking the eggs into a separate container to ensure that a bad one doesn't ruin the others and insists that the tomatoes used for the sauce need to be full of flavour and very sweet.

SERVES 4

Tomato Sauce:

400g perfumed, fragrant tomatoes
  or cherry tomatoes

Salt and pepper

75ml olive oil

240g Robiola (or a 50/50 mix of ricotta and mascarpone) ie 60g per person. Fresh herbs such as parsley or marjoram, chopped

Frittata:

8 fresh eggs

Salt and pepper to taste

80g Grana Padano, grated

Handful of field herbs or cicoria,
  chopped

20ml olive oil

A few small edible flowers (optional)

To make the tomato sauce, immerse the tomatoes in boiling water for 30 seconds. Remove and put in iced water to cool and then peel. If using large tomatoes, remove the seeds, but leave them if using cherry tomatoes. Put in a blender with the salt, pepper and olive oil. Blitz and pass through a sieve. Leave to cool.

Add pepper, but no salt, to the creamy Robiola along with whatever herbs are to hand. Place the cheese in a piping bag and pipe a ring of cheese on to a plate. Then make a ring of tomato sauce.

To make the frittata, beat the eggs in a bowl. Add the salt, pepper, cheese and herbs, and mix together with a fork. Heat a non-stick pan, add the oil, then the eggs. Stir the eggs around with a fork as it starts to set in places, so that all the liquid is mixed in, but as soon as it starts to firm up, stop stirring. When it's set turn it over and cook for a further minute then turn out of the pan and serve with the fresh tomato sauce and Robiola cheese. Decorate with fresh herbs and edible flowers if wished.

Wine suggestion: White – Lugana Brolettino, Cà dei Frati (Turbiana)

Torta di Pere con Salsa di Cioccolato
Pear Torta with Chocolate Sauce

Thanks to the addition of lemon zest and vanilla, cooking this torta creates a delicious fragrance in the kitchen. Note that Paolo never adds water to pastry.

SERVES 6-8

Pastry:

150g unsalted butter

250g plain flour

Grated zest of 1 lemon

Seeds from 1 vanilla pod
or powdered vanilla

125g caster sugar

3 medium egg yolks

4-5 pears

2 tablespoons cocoa powder

Chocolate sauce:

200g dark chocolate

100ml cream

Icing sugar (optional)

Pastry cream:

500g full fat milk

Vanilla

Lemon rind (to be discarded)

4 egg yolks

125g caster sugar

2 tablespoons cornflour
in a large bowl

To make the pastry, rub the butter into the flour and mix with the zest, vanilla, sugar and eggs so everything is nicely combined. Avoid overworking. Rest for 6-8 hours in the fridge.

To make the pastry cream, put the milk, vanilla and the lemon rind into a pan and bring to the boil.

In a large bowl, whisk the egg yolks and sugar together.

When fully mixed, add the cornflour. When the milk has come to the boil, remove the lemon rind and pour half the milk into the cornflour and mix until absorbed and then pour in the other half and mix completely. When fully mixed, return to the pan, bring back to the boil over a very gentle heat, stirring continuously. Boil for 15 seconds and then remove from the heat. Leave to cool, put into a bowl and refrigerate.

Peel the pears, cut into quarters and core. Roll out the pastry and fill a greased 22cm tart case leaving a good 2cm of pastry beyond the height of the case. Put about 4 spoons of the pastry cream over the bottom of the pastry case and place the pear quarters on top. Place the remaining pastry cream over the pears and fill in the gaps between the pears leaving some pieces of fruit exposed. Sprinkle abundantly with the cocoa powder.

Pre-heat the oven to 175 - 180°C. Roll out another pastry disk and cut out a circle smaller than the tart bottom and place over the top and fold over the pastry edges to seal. Bake for 50 minutes. Check that the top (which was at the bottom of the baking tin) is completely cooked. If not, place back in the oven for a few minutes until it is. Leave to cool slightly, turn out gently and position upside down.

To make the chocolate sauce, very gently melt the chocolate and cream in a bowl over a pan of simmering water ensuring that the water stays clear of the bowl, and mix together. Cut the tart into slices and serve with a spoonful of warm sauce and a sprinkle of icing sugar (if using).

Wine suggestion: Dessert – Banyuls or Marsala Vecchio Samperi Ventennale, Marco de Bartoli (Grillo)

Grazie di Curtatone

The hamlet of Grazie is on the bank of the River Mincio and is the departure point for '*I Barcaioli del Mincio,*' the boat trips that are especially popular at sunset. The river and the Parco del Mincio are well-known places to spot herons and grebes.

A few metres from the water is the Santuario di Santa Maria delle Grazie. Once a year the large square in front of it, which is usually a car park, is the venue for an international street painting festival, which, for a few days, attracts as many visitors as the Santuario does pilgrims.

Locanda delle Grazie
Fernando Aldighieri and Daniela Bellintani

via San Pio X, 2
46010 Grazie di Curtatone
T: +39 0376 348 038

Opening hours: 12.30 – 14.30;
19.30 – 22.30
Closed: Tues and Wed
Holidays: a few days at
the start of Jan, a few days
between the end of Jun and
the start of Jul, 2 weeks in Aug

Fernando Aldighieri wasn't the first teenager to solve the problem of his need for cash by finding a job as a waiter. But from that almost accidental beginning, restaurant work has become an all-consuming way of life. He moved from front of house to the kitchen in 1978, and has been there ever since.

As well as everywhere else. Because as Daniela, his wife and colleague, explains, "he does the work of four people. If something needs to be done somewhere, then he's there."

He arrives at work in the morning with a spring in his step. Or rather a bound. He loves the start of the day when there's "movement and mirth, and lots to do," as he puts it. When he's not dashing off to buy produce, checking deliveries and dealing with surprise problems, he's organising his team, making pasta or baking loaves.

The edible welcome at Locanda delle Grazie isn't just home-made bread, grissini and *schiacciatine*, but a glass of fizz too. Sometimes a sparkling Chardonnay from Lake Garda, or perhaps one from the Oltrepò Pavese. Fernando likes to vary them. He even has an own label Lambrusco Mantovano.

And that's apt as the menu is proudly Mantuan, or more accurately "*la cucina familiare mantovana*". Which is why you'll have a choice of local *salumi*, *sorbir d'agnoli*, *tortelli di zucca*, freshwater fish and *risotto alla pilota*.

Not only is the food of its place but so too is the interior. The couple asked an artist friend to paint something that guests would remember. She was

keen to produce a work that reflected where they are, so created painted panels featuring the Mincio river and its reserve with herons, egrets and fields. "From that," says Daniela, "came the green furniture and table linens."

And a burst of colour and cosiness comes from the flowery tablecloths, cushion covers and the crocheted menu covers, all of which Daniela chooses because they're handmade and unique. "We shouldn't aspire to be 'standard'," she says, and expanding on this philosophy, she adds, "Nobody is the same as someone else — even our faults can be beautiful."

This calm tolerance is unsurprising when you know that the three books that have had the biggest influence on her are Richard Bach's Jonathan Livingstone Seagull, Saint-Exupéry's Le Petit Prince and Herman Hesse's Siddhartha. This trio of philosophical and spiritual classics have been constants throughout her life.

But as well as fiction and philosophy, she likes factual research, especially finding out about the history of any house she's lived in — which naturally includes this one. There's even a brief written piece on what she has discovered about the building inside the menu.

That sense of discovery inspired her in other ways, too. The *locanda* is on the edge of the Piazzale Santuario. In fact it was seeing the Santuario di Santa Maria delle Grazie from the upstairs window of the flat above the restaurant that convinced Daniela that this would be her home.

It was a quick decision — a lot quicker certainly than the one that brought her and Fernando together. But Fernando was tenacious, even asking her to go to Polynesia with him. She told him it wasn't possible. But he wasn't going to take no for an answer so she agreed to meet him in Paris on his way back to Italy. He arrived at Charles de Gaulle airport wearing tan-enhancing white linen and tennis shoes — in the middle of a January snowstorm. They wined and dined on the Eiffel Tower with the lights of Paris below them.

But that was a long time ago and they've been a very happy team for many years since then. Daniela loves her work in the restaurant, especially the variety it involves. "The important thing is to believe in what you do," she says, while picking additional blooms to perfect a beautiful flower arrangement for a group who are celebrating a wedding anniversary.

For Fernando it's also about respect: respect for everyone he works with and for. He is a firm believer that it must be mutual — and he carries that belief

Above left: Fernando and his team busy making pasta

through to cost and quality. "We all need to pay the right price for produce," he insists, "and avoid intensive breeding and cultivation."

Which is why many of his suppliers, such as the fishermen he's worked with for decades, have become real friends. But then he's never been fickle; he even dislikes throwing food away, although there's a reason for that. "My father weighed 42kg when he returned from a prisoner of war camp," he says, "so it was impossible to not finish your food in front of him." Obviously, Fernando doesn't have a problem with diners not clearing their plates, but they are offered the chance to take uneaten food (and unfinished wine) home with them. As he says, "Eat it tomorrow, or give it to the dog, but don't throw food away."

On a warm summer's evening, there's a sign on the front door "*Siamo in Cortile*" which tells you to head round the back to the courtyard. There, the jasmine-fragranced terrace is abuzz with the sound of happy diners. Listen carefully and in the background through the kitchen window you'll hear Fernando calling out orders and orchestrating service.

But it's also highly likely that Fernando himself will serve something to you. Perhaps he'll fillet a fish at your table while sharing a few laughs and stories. He still loves that social side of his job. After all, it started with waiting tables.

Risotto alla Pilota
Rice Miller's Risotto

This is an old and traditional Mantuan risotto that extraordinarily doesn't require any stirring because it was made by the workers in the rice mills who weren't able to stop work to cook for very long. Fernando loves this local rice dish so much that he says he could "even eat it for breakfast."

SERVES 4

400g Vialone Nano rice

Salt

50g unsalted butter

280g minced pork or sausage meat

120g pancetta, finely chopped

Finely chopped garlic, to taste

Pepper

Mix of ground cinnamon, nutmeg and coriander, to taste

50g Grana Padano, grated, and more for serving (if you like)

Add the rice to a litre of salted water, bring to the boil and leave to cook for 7 minutes. Drain the water and return the rice to the warm pan. Cover with a muslin cloth and lid and leave for 20 minutes.

In another pan put the butter and 200ml water and cook the pork, pancetta and garlic. Break it up with a wooden spoon, so that some large bits stick together.

Drain the meat and add to the rice. Season, sprinkle over the spices, add the cheese and mix well with a wooden spoon. Serve with grated Grana Padano (if using).

Wine suggestion: Red – Granrosso del Vicariato, Quistello (Lambrusco Ruberti, Ancellotta)

Tagliatelle con Anitra
Duck Tagliatelle

Fernando makes his own pasta for this, but you can, of course, use dried tagliatelle. This is one of the most popular primo dishes on his menu.

SERVES 6-8

3 white onions, finely chopped	1.25kg duck
1 stick celery, finely chopped	1 litre red wine
4 carrots, finely chopped	Grana Padano, to taste
50ml olive oil	
1 sprig of rosemary, finely chopped	**Pasta:**
5 juniper berries	8 eggs
5 cloves garlic, finely chopped	700g 00 flour
Salt	

Heat the oil in a large saucepan and cook the vegetables, juniper and garlic. Add the salt and then the duck. Brown the duck on all sides. Pour over the red wine. Cover and leave to cook for at least 2 hours on a gentle heat. Every so often turn the duck over and add water if it dries out.

While the duck is cooking make the pasta. Cover and leave to rest for 30 minutes. Roll out thinly and cut into tagliatelle.

Use a fork to check that the duck is cooked. When the meat falls away, take the duck out of the pan, discard the skin and remove the meat from the carcass and cut into wide julienne strips. Return the meat to the pan and mix with the cooking liquid.

Cook the pasta, then add to the sauce and heat until piping hot. Serve with grated Grana Padano to your liking.

Wine suggestion: Red – Montevolpe Rosso, Bertagna (Merlot, Cabernet, Corvina)

Isola Dovarese

Driving around the corner and entering Isola Dovarese's main square, the cinematic Piazza Matteotti for the first time, elicits an "ooh" from most people.

But despite the grand setting, the feel of the town harks back to a simpler time: exuberant kids playing on bikes after school stop by the water tap for a drink or a splash, infrequent cars drive through carefully and everyone finds time to wave, or stop to chat. Even more reminiscent of halcyon days is that lots of people leave their keys in their car.

Caffè La Crepa
Franco, Fausto and Federico Malinverno

Piazza Matteotti, 13
26031 Isola Dovarese
T: +39 0375 396 161
W: caffelacrepa.it

Opening hours: 12.30 –
14.30; 19.30 – 22.30
Closed: Mon and Tues
Holidays: 2 weeks in Jan,
first week of Jul and
2 weeks in Sep

Don't let the name fool you. Caffè La Crepa is so very much more than your usual café. It's a trattoria held in high regard by critics and huge affection by the locals — but it's the not-so locals who have turned it into one of Lombardy's essential culinary destinations.

We can be pretty sure that Giuseppe and Elda Malinverno, who opened their simple neighbourhood osteria in 1951 on the opposite side of Piazza Matteotti, weren't thinking ahead to such plaudits. They were just trying to serve good, simple fare. Giuseppe would catch local fish from the Oglio River. His wife would cook it. If you popped in for a drink and a game of cards with your mates, you might have found salt cod fritters or meatballs on the menu, but nothing fancy because Elda in particular was juggling the demands of running a business and raising her sons Franco and Fausto.

Inevitably, the boys lent a hand. In fact the brothers have been helping out in the Malinverno family restaurant for as long as they can remember. But then, in those days so did the customers — and not just with the meals. Decades later the brothers still talk to locals who reminisce about going to their parents' osteria and helping to dress the youngsters and get them to school.

That may have changed but the culinary themes have remained constant. "We're on the Oglio River so we've always served freshwater fish," says Franco. "For a long time the fishmonger had very few customers like us, but the Oglio, the Mincio, the Po and Lake Garda are our gastronomic culture." He's forged close ties with local producers and when possible prefers to go to his suppliers rather than have everything delivered to his kitchen.

Which means that should you be interested in the provenance of an item or ingredient, Fausto will gladly tell all. However, suppliers' particulars don't appear on the menu because the brothers feel that starting with excellent produce is one thing, but making it into plates of memorable food is their responsibility.

But not everyone comes for food. Although people travel from far away to eat here, the locals still pop in for a coffee or glass of wine, and are warmly welcomed. The brothers have always maintained strong relationships with their neighbours (which may be why Sunday morning sees the bar at the entrance full of elderly locals having a pre-Mass sharpener, or a wine elevenses).

But it's as a trattoria that Caffè la Crepa has gained a fine reputation that extends far beyond its immediate surroundings. And that goes for the staff as well as the food. For example, Fausto is skilled enough to check that all

is OK without clumsily asking a direct question. And clarity is important to him. "Clients are spending their hard-earned cash with us so everything must be clear, including the prices. There should never be any surprises," he says. He's also perfectly happy if people don't want a full meal but just one course. "We're used to that and won't think badly of you even if you only want a dessert." But then one dessert in particular, ice cream is a big part of the story here.

Back in 1976 the brothers opened an ice cream shop and the *gelato* word spread far beyond the confines of their town. Maybe it's an Italian marketing strategy: people hear about your amazing ice cream, travel to have some and then return for a full meal.

Federico, Franco's son, jokes that he started helping out with the ice cream as soon as he was born. He's certainly a big part of the business now. However, his route to working in the restaurant was along a less-than-obvious educational path: he studied philosophy at the University of Bologna, returning to work in the trattoria at the weekends.

He still sees the division of the week — concentrating completely on one thing and then on another — as being beneficial. This may even have played a part in his thesis, An Idea of Development: a Local Micro-Economy, on the sustainable development of small towns. "Some people think that philosophy is removed from reality but this is a practical philosophy," he points out. "It's enabled me to apply the big principles of the world to my daily life. You have to put everything into your own context."

In order to do just that he followed up with a Masters in History and Food Culture which involved travelling around Europe because "I wanted to properly live the gastronomy: mushroom hunting, vineyards, markets, foie gras. In two months I ate in 40 restaurants. It was very useful."

Opposite top left: Fausto

Opposite top right: Franco

Opposite bottom left: Federico

Whether it's Federico's academic training or something innate, he does repeatedly challenge orthodoxies; he's an intriguing mixture of thinker and doer. But he's not the only one who is open to change. "Both my father and my uncle are very open-minded," he says. For instance, Franco gladly accepts *stagiaires* in his kitchen because "they get us to think differently about how things are done — so we learn too. It's not one-way; it's an exchange." Which is rather delightful given that "my father is very, very attached to his territory. The kitchen is his domain."

More than anything, perhaps, Franco believes strongly that "people have tastes in their minds that were formed in childhood — and they're the tastes that they continue to seek out." And on a beautifully sunny Sunday, there are a lot of children perhaps about to have that very formative experience as a large ready-to-celebrate christening party settles in. Around them the place is buzzing. La Crepa is packed for lunch. There are only two empty seats and they're opposite the two lone diners. But they too fit in just fine. This place attracts a broad mix of people: lovebirds, families, cyclists in full lycra and three elderly ladies, resplendently dolled up and tucking in with gusto and questions.

Franco comes out of the kitchen and talks to them and everyone he knows. He's genuinely interested in what people have to say and stops to answer questions on the daily specials. He's not seeking praise or applause. He simply knows that lots of friends are in and wants to exchange a few words with them.

Two hours after arriving, the big christening party starts speeches with serious applauding and cheering, the sort that comes after a good, wine-enhanced lunch with nearest and dearest. You can't fail to have a happy childhood with such an affectionate and light-hearted start.

Towards the end of lunch as everything starts to slow down and some people depart, the mood has changed a little. There's a feeling, when the lingerers take a second coffee and perhaps a grappa, that all is well with the world and that friendships have another happy moment to add to their archive.

And all this in a place still touchingly called a caffè. It's evolved over the years from the simplest of starts to attract international acclaim but the three Malinverno men have ensured that Caffè La Crepa has never lost its soul — the soul of the neighbourhood osteria their family opened in 1951.

Insalata di Faraona alla Stefani
Guinea Fowl Salad

This salad is based on an ancient recipe by Bartolomeo Stefani, who published L'Arte de Ben Cucinare in Mantua in 1662. Today it's perfect as an antipasto or as a light secondo. You may well find it easier to use a whole guinea fowl and keep the spare meat for something else.

SERVES 4

Half a guinea fowl
4 knobs of butter
A few sage leaves and sprigs of rosemary
Olive oil
Salt and pepper
Salad leaves
80g candied citrus fruit, diced

20g raisins
8 Datterini tomatoes, quartered
Extra virgin olive oil
Traditional balsamic vinegar

Pre-heat the oven to 160°C.

Place the guinea fowl in a baking dish with the butter, herbs, oil, salt and pepper. Cook in the oven for an hour covered with foil to keep the steam in so that the meat becomes succulent. Once cooked, remove the meat from the bone and break into bite-size pieces.

In a separate bowl put the salad leaves, candied fruit, raisins and tomatoes. Season and add oil and vinegar to taste. Mix in the guinea fowl and serve.

Wine suggestion: White – Malvasia Vendemmia Tardiva, Massimiliano Croci (100% Malvasia). To be served cold at 14°C.

Torta Sabbiosa
Sand Cake

A finely crumbed cake which is a popular light dessert but works well as a mid-afternoon pick-me-up too. It's served at La Crepa with mascarpone cream, and sometimes chocolate ice cream.

SERVES 8

½ tsp yeast

2 tbsp tepid milk

3 eggs

250g caster sugar

350g potato starch (often sold as potato flour)

200g butter, plus extra for greasing

Icing sugar, for decoration

A mix of whipped cream, mascarpone, sugar and vanilla (optional)

Grease a 21cm cake tin, and pre-heat the oven to 170°C. Dissolve the yeast in the milk, then add to the eggs and sugar. Whisk together with an electric whisk until the sugar has dissolved and the mix is pale in colour.

Separately mix the potato starch and butter together until it forms a soft creamy mixture. Add this to the eggs and sugar and mix it all together with the whisk.

Put into the prepared cake tin, place on a baking tray and cook for 50 minutes. Check that it is done with a skewer. Remove from the oven and leave to cool in the tin. Remove from the tin, sieve over some icing sugar to taste. Serve with vanilla mascarpone cream (if you like).

Wine suggestion: Federico prefers a beer with this, namely, Lune, Baladin.

Mandello del Lario

Mandello del Lario is a small town on Lake Como with a picture postcard *imbarcadero*. Not too touristy, it has some good cafés and ice cream shops and smiling residents. It's probably best known for being the home of the Moto Guzzi factory, which has been producing the legendary eponymous motorbikes since the 1920s.

Apparently back in the 1960s, workers from the Moto Guzzi factory would head to the lake at six in the evening on their bicycles, and with their towels and soaps would wash up before heading home.

Osteria Sali e Tabacchi
Gabriele Lafranconi and Giuliana Valpolini

Piazza San Rocco, 3
Località Maggiana
Mandello del Lario
T: +39 0341 733715
W: osteriasalietabacchi.it

Opening hours: 10-00-
14.00; 18.00-24.00
Closed: Mon and Tues
Holidays: first 2 weeks Jan;
2 weeks after Ferragosto

Fittingly for a cartographer, it was a map that guided him. Surprisingly for an Italian chef, it was a gastronomic map of France. At the time, Gabriele Lafranconi was a food-fixated editor of travel guides in Milan. He loved both working in, and eating his way round the big city. But his world was changing. He was drawing maps by hand at a time when everything was becoming digitised. What wasn't changing was his preoccupation with food.

Which conveniently coincided with his sister's struggles back in his home town — or, more accurately, his home. Big supermarket competition was blackening the clouds above her small food shop, the one their parents had set up in 1948. In the same building, Gabriele's father had made bread while his mother ran the shop and cooked simple meals in the bread oven. But one sibling's famine is another's feast and Gabriele and his wife Giuliana saw an opportunity to help her — and themselves. First they quickly sorted out the practicalities of their long-standing wish to leave their office jobs and do something together that involved welcoming people. Then they took over the family premises.

Fast forward the best part of twenty years and they now run an osteria with a distinctly neighbourhood feel that harks back to a simpler time. From the outside it looks like a casual bar, and indeed the locals like to pop in for a coffee or even a morning glass of wine. The postie stops to chat to those inside and on a sunny day catches up, in a pretty leisurely manner, with those sitting outside. It's an unassuming and understated place.

But if it wasn't an obvious and straightforward route for Gabriele and Giuilana to work with each other, that's nothing compared to their journey as a couple. Let's just say that they met at primary school but it took them a decade or two to get together.

But by 1999 they'd had a family and were eager to start their new adventure. They quickly revamped the family premises, changing the bread-making area into what is now the dining room (although the table where Gabriele's father used to make the bread is still there) and finding local artisans to fit out the bar area. Then they opened their osteria.

Ideas of what to cook had long been developing in Gabriele's mind, "I've been a member of Slow Food from the very beginning and that was the motor that drove me on," he says.

That and simple food that the couple knew was good. Gabriele had grown up eating rice and fish. And sure enough, even now there's always fish antipasti on the menu — local fish, from Lake Como. "I love cooking lake fish, especially *lavarello*. I think it has a delicious, almost hazelnutty taste," he says. But he understands why some people think lake fish taste 'muddy'. "I'm not so keen on the fish that feed from the bottom such as tench. The flesh of those that live and eat higher up is much more delicate. But I've changed the minds of lots of people who think badly of lake fish. When they try *lavarello*, cooked simply in the oven, they say it's as good as sea bass," he smiles. He even goes fishing with the Lake Como pros when time permits.

For someone who is such a supporter and fan of local gastronomy, his knowledge of foreign cuisines is impressive. Of course, as you'd expect of someone who worked in travel publishing, he loves exploring. In fact before running their own business, Gabriele and Giuliana used to scoot off on their Moto Guzzi exploring Turkey or Kurdistan or spending a couple of months in Greece and continually feeling the pull of the French hexagon. But then Gabriele's always had a soft spot for France.

In fact he was inspired by bistros he'd been to there. "I like places that welcome all types of people," he explains. "Given that there's no longer anywhere to socialise in this village I wanted somewhere that was informal and open to all."

And that is indeed what they've created. If you opt to stay overnight in their delightful B&B you may be lucky enough to have some delicious home-made cake for breakfast, or perhaps even have a late-night chat over a coffee and grappa with the couple when things are slowing down. Listening to their tales of travelling — with and without their two young daughters — is a revelation: life-enhancing stories of happy, simple holidays, staying on campsites and searching out the very best food.

Above left: Gabriele chatting with the lake fishermen

Above right: Giuliana

Giuliana still thinks that welcoming and getting to know people who come from other countries is one of the best parts of her job. She explains that the people who come from abroad are those who know about good food. Although Sali e Tabacchi is only a short — but appetite-justifying — walk up from the waterfront, it's not a passing trade place so such visitors have clearly done their research.

You may be surprised to hear Gabriele, in his softly spoken, gently determined way, talk about how against globalisation he is. Not for narrow, parochial reasons but because he laments the eroding of differences. "Milan has lost a bit of its identity, a bit of its 'Milano-ness,'" he explains. "I remember when people used to speak in the Milanese dialect and you don't really hear that anymore. Things evolve, and that's right. But I think diversity is an asset and holding on to your cultural identity is important."

He concedes that this may be a rather romantic aspect of gastronomy but says the best compliment he receives is people saying a dish he's served them brings back certain half-buried memories. Perhaps that's why he loves serving big family tables at Sunday lunchtimes.

Gabriele didn't go to catering school. He learnt on the job, and he's very grateful to many of the people he worked alongside, including talented youngsters, like Stefano Binda who went on to gain a Michelin star and who taught him lots about professional cooking techniques. But Gabriele still believes that there are some things catering school can't teach you. "You can't learn about traditional tastes at school. Your own flavours come from your family imprints because your grandparents, aunts and parents all pass on these traditions."

Which may be why Gabriele and Giuliana work so closely with local producers and excitedly serve sliced bresaola or an excellent local cheese at *aperitivo* time. Gabriele may no longer be drawing maps but he's still guiding people around the culinary traditions of the Lakes.

Antipasto di Pesce di Lago
Lake Fish Antipasto

Gabriele's lake fish antipasto has four different parts including agoni in carpione (fried fish that are marinated in vinegar, wine, sugar, pepper and herbs). It's hard to get hold of a suitable variety of lake fish, unless you live near to a lake, but this is a flexible recipe, so use what's easy for you, and quantities that suit your appetite.

SERVES 6

Fish and salad

Mix 6-7 pieces (per person) of smoked fish with mixed salad leaves and some halved cherry tomatoes. Dress in extra virgin olive oil and vinegar. Add a handful of Taggiasche olives.

Fish pâté

1 shallot, chopped

Knob of butter for frying

130g mixed lake fish fillets, skin and bones carefully removed

Salt and white pepper

A few sprigs each of marjoram and thyme, finely chopped

10ml cognac

10g butter

10ml fresh cream

6 small slices of bread

In a non-stick pan, brown the shallot in a little butter. Cut the fish into pieces, add to the pan and brown lightly. Season, add the herbs then the cognac and let it reduce. Remove from the heat and add the butter so that it melts in the residual warmth. Leave to cool before blending finely and adding just the right amount of cream so that it doesn't become too loose. It should be a very fine mixture. Leave to cool and serve on toasted bread.

Fish with polenta

Take 1 fillet of small fish per person and lightly fry. Dress with oil and vinegar. Serve on a mound or wedge of polenta, to a size of your choosing. (Gabriele uses an ice cream scoop to measure his, and either serves it warm if freshly made, or grills it.)

**Wine suggestion: White – Solesta, La Costa
(Riesling Renano, Chardonnay, Incrocio Manzoni)**

Aspic di Frutta
Fruit Jellies

Giuliana always makes desserts at Osteria Sali e Tabacchi. Use whatever soft fruits are at their best for this dessert and do check your gelatine to ensure that you use the right amount for the quantity of liquid here.

SERVES 12

1 x 750ml bottle moscato

4 tbsp caster sugar

4 sheets gelatine

5 apricots

200g strawberries

200g raspberries

100g blackberries

2-3 small mint leaves per
  portion (optional)

Fruit or fruit coulis for serving
  (optional)

Put the wine and sugar in a pan, bring to the boil and leave for 10 minutes to burn off some of the alcohol, then remove from the heat. In the meantime, soften the gelatine in cold water. Add the gelatine to the wine and sugar mixture and stir until it has dissolved, then leave to cool.

Wash, prepare and, if necessary, cut the fruit into small pieces. Fill the moulds with fruit, and mint leaves if using. When the wine is cooled, pour it over the fruit until the moulds are almost full. Put the moulds in the fridge for several hours to set.

Serve with some fruit or even a coulis should you wish.

Wine suggestion: Dessert wine – either pair with the moscato used in the jelly or, as it's such a light dessert, accompany with some light home made biscuits or *pasticceria secca* with a Vertemate IGT Bianco Terrazze Retiche di Sondrio Passito (Traminer Aromatico, Riesling)

Mantua

The historical and architectural treasures of Mantova, as it's called in Italian, are well documented. A boat trip gives you the opportunity to see much of what the city has to offer from the water.

When you're not absorbing the history, the numerous porticoes make it possible to window shop sheltered from the weather, whatever the season. The Mantuans may say that they're quite reserved but ask for directions and they're more than likely to throw in some additional guidance, just to be helpful. They may even advise on their favourite place to have a glass of Lambrusco Mantovano.

La Tur dal Sücar
Giovanni Comparini

La Tur dal Sücar
via S Longino, 3
Mantua 46100
T: +39 0376 322 320

Opening hours:
07.00-13.00;
16.00-20.00
Closed: Mon

This renowned and popular *pasticceria* is owned by local baker Giovanni Comparini who started work as a pastry chef at the age of 14. This is his recipe for the classic crumbly almond torta of Mantua, *sbrisolona*, which is one of his best sellers. This was traditionally made with only cornmeal, but these days it's more common to include some wheat flour too.

Sbrisolona
Mantuan Almond Tart

250g cornmeal, finely ground
85g plain flour
160g unsalted butter
160g caster sugar
160g shelled almonds, roughly
   chopped

1 egg, beaten

Handful of unblanched
   almonds, for decoration
1 tbsp sugar, to finish

Mix the cornmeal and plain flour. Add the butter and rub together into coarse breadcrumbs. Add the caster sugar then the chopped almonds and finally the egg. The mixture will be crumbly and won't hang together.

Pre-heat the oven to 200°C.

Put into a 25cm round, greased tart tin and level out but don't press down or compact. Decorate with whole almonds.

Cook in the oven for around 60 minutes and remove when it is golden brown and a metal skewer comes out clean. Keep an eye on it to ensure that it doesn't catch, and cover with foil if necessary. Remove from the oven and sprinkle over the final spoon of sugar. Leave to cool and then break up with your hands to eat.

Bar Caravatti
Guido Giordani

Piazza Erbe
46100 Mantua
T: +39 0376 327 826

Opening hours:
Mon – Thurs and Sun
07.15 – 21.00;
Fri and Sat 07.15 – 24.00
Holidays: none

On a summer's Saturday night, Bar Caravatti is almost empty. At least it is inside. Outside, it's buzzing. The tables beneath the porticoes are full of people enjoying a balmy evening out — young couples with babies, partying professionals and groups of friends, all chatting to everyone they know who passes. This is Italy at its most sociable and appealing.

Guido Giordani, who runs the bar, explains that unlike in winter when there's a continuous flow of customers — from the morning coffee and pastries, via a quick *risino* (a popular sweet, rice-filled tartlet) to late-night carousing — in the summer there's a brief afternoon lull when people go swimming before returning to town for *aperitivi*.

And the early evening drink of choice here is a Caravatti, the secret recipe house vermouth served with seltzer and ice. There are three types: red, rosé (sweeter and less alcoholic) and white (dryer, light and citrusy), but the red is by far the best seller — probably because "lots of Mantuans don't know the others exist," says Guido. However, the bar's mirrors — mementoes from an earlier marketing experiment that didn't last — offer a clue. The classic accompaniment to the Caravatti is anchovies and butter on bread. But there's a choice of other *crostini*, and the obligatory array of crisps and nuts at *aperitivo* time.

Although requests for a Caravatti are constant, there's an interesting selection of wines by the glass, including some natural and biodynamic ones. The staff are very knowledgeable about them, but Max Orondoni is a real wine connoisseur. He's also an excellent barman: a welcoming smile, good banter with regulars and the ability to effortlessly multi-task. Rosa Visconti is impressive too. She came from Sicily to Mantua for love. That didn't last, but she did. She's gregarious and funny with beautiful eyes

that, judging from her extraordinary efficiency, sometimes seem to be in the back of her head.

The founders of Bar Caravatti were a family of immigrants whose name was spelt with one 't'. Was the bar's name a spelling mistake by the sign maker or a way of appearing more Italian? Who knows? Either way, the bar is now an essential part of the fabric of Mantua.

Top left: Max Orondoni entertaining regulars

Bottom left: Rosa Visconti

Bar Venezia
Marco Gialdi

Piazza Marconi, 9-10
46100 Mantua
T: +39 0376 321 509
W: barvenezia.it

Opening hours:
07.00 – 21.00
Open every day
except 25 Dec

Marco Gialdi, the owner of Bar Venezia, explains that it's the oldest bar in Mantua. "It's been here since about 1850," he says. "And the site was once a *pasticceria* where the *Torta Elvezia* was created." That Mantuan speciality — an almond cake with a creamy zabaglione filling — is no longer baked here, but it is served.

As are all the usual Italian bar drinks and snacks. But then Bar Venezia is open all day, so there's a steady flow of morning coffee drinkers, followed by the pre-lunch *aperitivi* crowd. Then there's a nod to afternoon tea before the working day finishes with the evening *aperitivi* rush.

Marco manages his team throughout these different waves. He's spent his working life in the hospitality business, and it has taken him to many places, but he always feels the pull of his home town. "Mantua is a magnificent city," he enthuses. "We Mantuans appreciate culture and the good things in life."

Oh, and if you're thinking that one of Mantua's longest established bars is named after another Italian city, think again. "Before 1900 it was owned by people called Veneziani. In fact many locals still call it Bar del Veneziano."

And it's very popular with the locals. Stand at the bar even briefly and you'll hear a stream of "ciao Marco" greetings as the regulars come and go. There's always a good choice of wines, including Dom Perignon by the glass, as well as old school favourites: Americano, Negroni, and gin and tonic, albeit with a range of over 30 types of gin and a selection of tonics, which the barman will help you to choose. Ask for a beer on a hot day and the glass is chilled with an ice cube first.

Or you could grab a quick coffee at the bar and opt for a *resentin* (a few drops of grappa to "rinse out" the coffee cup). "It's an idea from Verona

but popular here too," explains Marco. If you prefer to avoid the barside banter, take a seat for a coffee and a *cornetto* or a fruit smoothie. "People who come here like to sit down", says Marco. "We don't attract the crazy crowd".

Milan

The city of Milan is much more than the capital of the region of Lombardy. It's a major European business centre and packs a powerful design and style punch.

But it's not just finance and fashion. The world-leading La Scala opera house has been a stronghold of musical excellence for centuries, not only for the great and good of Milan but for the discerning from much further afield.

With its extraordinary duomo and well-curated exhibitions at places such as La Triennale, not to mention head-turning shop window displays, Milan has something for everyone.

Il Camparino
Orlando Chiari

Galleria Vittorio Emanuele angolo Piazza Duomo, 21 20121 Milan T: +39 02 8646 4435 W: camparino.it

Opening hours: 07.15 – 20.40
Closed: Mon
Holidays: 25 Dec

Gaspare Campari's Caffè Campari, to the right of Milan's Galleria entrance, was founded in 1867, quickly becoming the meeting place for the city's great and good. In 1915, an offshoot was set up opposite: Il Camparino, a café where you could grab a quick coffee or drink while standing up. Standing on either side of the entrance to the Galleria, there were now two cafés attracting Milan's influential and elite.

Caffè Campari no longer exists, but the Camparino still holds its own. Today, you don't have to lean against the bar appreciating the Mazzucotelli chandeliers, the Angelo d'Andrea mosaics or the general Art Nouveau style. There is now the less cultural but more entertaining option of relaxing at a table outside watching the passers-by: Milanese head turners, tourists following flag-holding leaders or impassive high-end shoppers.

There's a choice of coffees, wines and cocktails but caffeine or Campari are the default options here: a Campari soda or a Negroni perhaps? The favourite drink of Orlando Chiari who runs this Milan institution is the house 'Mosaico' which includes vodka, dry martini, sweet sparkling wine, oh, and the bitter red aperitif, of course.

There's a skill to serving bitters correctly; in fact it's a skill on which Il Camparino's reputation was built. There were all sorts of explanations given for this renown: the tall thin glasses, the (always correct) temperature and the precision with which bar staff would add a mere squirt of water to rest on top. Orlando explains that the bar still has a machine in its cellar that makes soda water and acts as a perfect siphon.

The staff are seasoned pros and know that usually, as one puts it, "the people at the bar are regulars and those sitting outside are visitors from

around the world. It's a good mix." But when the suited businessmen need to sit down, they're handed a drinks list within seconds.

As for the aperitif that gives Il Camparino its name, Orlando's opinion, predictably, is that "a classic *aperitivo* is something bitter, and Campari was created here in Milano so it's no surprise that it's so popular". It's hard to disagree given the quantity his customers get through, but then he does serve 2,000 people on an average day. Who get through well over 4,000 bottles of Campari a year.

Opposite top: Orlando Chiari

Erba Brusca
Alice Delcourt and Danilo Ingannamorte

Alzaia Naviglio Pavese 286
20142 Milan
T: +39 02 8738 0711
W: erbabrusca.it

Opening hours: 12.30 –
14.30; 20.00 – 22.30
Closed: Mon and Tues
Holidays: 1 – 21 Jan

Our story starts with Danilo Ingannamorte cycling along the Milan-Pavia road and never being able to resist stopping at Osteria del Tubbetto. It had been there for years; he liked the atmosphere and he loved the live music.

But then Danilo knows a good osteria when he sees one. He's been working in them since the age of 14, through both school and university, in kitchens and front of house. He enjoys both but it's his love of wine that has seen him focus on the latter.

In fact it was wine that led Danilo to Alice Delcourt. They had met doing an Associazione Italiana Sommelier course, and occasionally ran into each other at wine tastings. When Danilo chose the former Osteria del Tubbetto as the site for his new restaurant he needed a chef. He'd heard good things about the small restaurant where Alice was working so went along with his business partner. The rest is history.

Alice's route to Strada Alzaia Naviglio Pavese in Milan was considerably more circuitous than Danilo's. She has an English mother and a French father, and was partly home-schooled in the States. But it was Italy that started her thinking about food differently. At 18 she stayed with an uncle in Bologna. He took her out for an espresso and she had a moment of revelation. "I'd never had a coffee like it," she says. "I'd been drinking hazelnut lattes at home and so I had no idea. It opened my mind up to food for the first time."

But not the last. The discoveries continued when her university sent her to Florence on an exchange programme as part of her political science and Italian studies. The woman she stayed with "cooked the most amazing things on the smallest oven. I found it so exciting and I really got into it. I'd make time to cycle to a restaurant where they'd show me how to make gnocchi. I just loved it all."

Alice had considered careers in public health, food or agriculture, but she gradually realised that "it always came back to food." There was, however, still a lot she didn't know so she worked hard and gained a wide variety of experiences — from catering on a boat off Panama, to small restaurants in Milan to the "cool and exciting" River Café in London. "I loved Rose Gray and Ruth Rogers," she says. "They were my inspiration. I loved their simple approach."

Danilo, meanwhile, wanted his new place to be "casual but with good food." He'd loved the vibe from places as diverse as New York, Spain and the Low Countries. He loves France and the ambience of Parisian bistros. And he wanted the food to have soul. "Cooking everything sous vide is a bit soulless," he says.

Which can't be said of this pair. The couple work closely with local suppliers, and then of course there's their *orto*, their kitchen garden, which may not allow them to be self-sufficient but it provides enough for self-satisfaction.

As does the menu. It's short, but Alice has worked in enough kitchens to know that "if you have a huge menu, you're always cutting corners; our menu's as big as it can be without compromising quality." There's also a

Opposite top: Danilo chatting to a neighbour

Opposite centre: Danilo and Alice

Opposite bottom: the vegetable garden

popular 'blind' menu. "You don't have to think about that one," says Danilo. "Of course you do have to be willing to try new things," he smiles.

His chef clearly agrees. "Other people get to know places through photography, literature or whatever their passion is, but I do it through food," she says. "And I love being a foreigner here; I'm excited about the traditions that make Italian food so amazing, but I'm not constricted by them."

Traditional Lombard specialities feature on the menu, although the pair is open to influences from just about everywhere. "You get inspired by tastes or flavours. That's why travel is so important and why it's important to eat, and work, in places that are not high end — to see what you can do with basic ingredients," says Alice. Danilo loves France, so they have French cheeses on the menu, while Alice loves Lebanese and Middle Eastern food, "which is what I think is closest to Italian food." But she's not going to rattle the saucepans for the sake of it. "*Pizzoccheri* is always on our menu in the winter. You can't change *pizzoccheri*. It's perfect as it is."

But it's not just her constant drive to find new things and serve great things that drives Alice on. "It's also important that people come and have a nice time because I've had the best times in my life around a table," she says. Alice never wanted Erba Brusca to just be about her food.

So it's a good job that Danilo is holding up his side of the deal. Along with a wine list of which he is very proud (his personal preferences are for French whites and Nebbiolo-based reds) there's also the music. Danilo is a big fan

of vinyl — the album playing is displayed in front of the till — and once played harmonica in a band called The Bronze Brothers ("like the Blues Brothers but tanned").

As for the unusual name of the former Osteria del Tubbetto, Danilo reflected on this for a long time. He wanted something that was linked to where they are. He also became fascinated by the *marcita* way of irrigating and farming grass that meant 11 harvests throughout the year. "It's a beneficial eco-system and a good example of how man can work without impoverishing but enhancing nature," he explains. *Erba brusca* is a wild sorrel that grew on the *marcita* so it seemed apt. Somewhat poetically, *erba brusca* started to grow in their garden once they'd named the restaurant.

Back on the Navigli, Danilo still cycles along the Milan-Pavia road, only these days he has Alice pedalling with him — and their twins in tow. Erba brusca isn't all that's happily flourishing in these parts.

Tarte Tatin con Pomodori Passiti e Melanzane al Forno
Tomato and Aubergine Tarte Tatin

Alice uses Perino or San Marzano tomatoes but the heating of the tomatoes concentrates their flavour, so this is also great for tomatoes that aren't as good as the ones used at Erba Brusca.

SERVES 6

Filling:

18 medium-large Perino or San Marzano tomatoes

2 cloves garlic, finely chopped

Salt

Olive oil

2 tbsp sugar

Small handful of thyme, chopped

3 medium aubergines, sliced about 1cm thick

Handful of basil leaves, chopped

Pastry:

250g flour

30g Parmesan, grated

145g cold butter, cut into cubes

2 small eggs, beaten

Caramel:

2 tbsp sugar

1 tbsp water and lemon juice

10g butter

Basil and thyme, chopped, to garnish

Fresh cheese, to accompany

6 x 11cm round baking tins, greased

Pre-heat the oven to 100°C.

Cut the tomatoes in half lengthwise and season with the garlic, salt, oil, the sugar and half the thyme. Put them in a baking pan, cut side up, and cook in the oven for 4 hours.

Meanwhile, cover the aubergines with salt, leave to drain for about 2 hours, then dry with kitchen paper. Once the tomatoes are done, take them out and turn the oven up to 170°C. Put the aubergines in a non-stick baking tin with a drizzle of oil and season with the basil and the rest of the thyme. Cook for 20 minutes.

To make the pastry, rub the flour, Parmesan and butter together to resemble breadcrumbs; add the eggs and knead. Rest the pastry in the fridge for 30 minutes.

To make the caramel, heat the sugar in a small saucepan with the water and lemon juice. When it darkens remove from the heat. Add the butter and mix well. Divide the caramel into the baking tins, then place the tomato halves, cut side down, the aubergine slices and finally a disc of pastry. Bake these on a tray in the oven for 15 minutes at 170°C.

When the pastry is done, and while they are still hot, turn them upside down on a plate to remove. Season with thyme, basil and serve with fresh cheese on the side.

Wine suggestion: Rosé – 'A Vita IGT Rosato (Gaglioppo)

Parfait al Cioccolato Fondente Olio Extra Vergine e Fleur de Sel
Chocolate Parfait with Extra Virgin Olive Oil and Fleur de Sel

Alice says that this is very simple but "it's important to respect the temperature of the chocolate. If it's too cold when you incorporate it into the egg whites, it will stiffen up and become lumpy; if it's too hot, it melts the whites. Otherwise it's easy peasy."

SERVES 8

140g sugar

150g egg whites

300g dark chocolate, melted and slightly cooled

500ml cream, whipped to soft peaks

Freezer-proof dish approx. 33cm x 26cm x 5cm deep

Cocoa powder

Fleur de sel

Extra virgin olive oil

Put the sugar and egg whites in a bowl over a pan of simmering water, bring them to a heat of between 50-60°C and beat to soft peaks. Fold the melted chocolate into this mixture gently with a plastic spatula in three batches, making sure not to knock out the air incorporated into the whites. Gently fold in the whipped cream.

Spread it out in a dish and freeze for at least 6 hours.

To serve, cut into 8 portions, leave to temper for a few minutes and serve with cocoa powder, fleur de sel and extra virgin olive oil sprinkled over the top to taste.

Wine suggestion: Sweet red – Moscato di Scanzo, Azienda Agricola Biava (Moscato di Scanzo)

L'Osteria del Treno
Angelo, Anna and Paolo Bissolotti

via S. Gregorio, 46/48
20124 Milan
T: +39 02 670 0479
W: osteriadeltreno.it

Opening hours: Mon – Fri
12.30 – 14.30, 20.00 – 24.00;
Sat and Sun 20.00 – 24.00
Closed: open every day
Holidays: 2 weeks in
Aug and a week between
Christmas and New Year

"My original idea was to set up an osteria serving traditional Italian foods made by the very best producers." Angelo Bissolotti is the first to admit that this approach is widespread today, but that was far from the case over 25 years ago when he opened L'Osteria del Treno a short walk from Milan's Centrale Station.

These days he runs the osteria with his two siblings, although, given their present occupation, all three of them have surprising employment histories. Angelo worked in a bank, then a juvenile prison. Anna was a primary school teacher. Paolo, meanwhile, was a high-flyer in the record business, dealing with the likes of Elton John, Genesis and Dire Straits. Between them they now hold the reins of arguably the most acclaimed traditional osteria in Milan.

But the Osteria del Treno story started in their childhood home where food was a passion and hard work was the norm — as were regular visits to traditional osterie for Angelo and Paolo from a very early age; their grandmother would send them round the local favourites to chivvy their grandfather into returning home for Sunday lunch.

Those memories are still vivid in Angelo's mind, as is his affection for the traditional Italian osteria. So what made him take the decision to become an *oste*? He was always enthusiastic about eating well, but, his brother Paolo explains, "He has the best understanding of food culture, and a broader knowledge of Italian gastronomy than anyone else I know."

Angelo was certainly one of the first people to join Slow Food Milan, and

there have always been around ten presidia on the menu, even though it changes pretty much monthly. At least the printed evening menu does.

At lunchtime it's a different matter. The daily specials are written on an easel at the end of the bar. It doesn't take long for a queue to form. A mix of smart office workers, casually dressed hipsters and very elegantly cardiganed and pearled women of a certain age, all turn up for something that is a lot more than mere midday sustenance. It's a ritual here, a daily pause to gather — hence the smiles and cheery acknowledgements.

Evenings are predictably quieter and in the back room (the one painted zabaglione yellow), it's usually pretty sedate in front of the now closed serving hatch. Among the old black-and-white photographs of Milan, diners linger, often making the most of a leisurely appreciation of the superb cheeses on offer. Perhaps a Lombard *caprino sott'olio*, a *Pannerone con mostarda di frutta* or a *Robiola di Pandino*. Angelo doesn't so much know the cheesemakers, as has seen some of them — such as Maria Chiara Onida of Il Boscasso — grow up.

On a Sunday night, however, it's not just the osteria that draws the regulars. In the large hall next door it's the weekly Milonga evening. Milonga is a form of tango, and for a nominal cost participants can have a drink and enjoy a buffet along with music and a few hours of dancing. The keenest dancers — the ones who rarely leave the floor — bring special shoes along. Between dances you might enjoy a hot pasta dish and survey the interior and exterior design of the hall itself. If you can get in, that is. Some nights Anna has to turn people away.

She's modest about her own dancing skills but praises Angelo's ability. In fact the three siblings are quite diffident so, if you want to discover the strengths of one of them, you'll have to ask the others. However, all three of them readily admit to being able to sing — so well in fact that Angelo and Paolo sing in a band together.

They also play cards — another tradition of the osteria, although, says Paolo, "ten years ago there were six tables of card players every day. Now there's one or two," which is why they occasionally help to make up the numbers.

In the course of more than a quarter of a century since Angelo set up his osteria, and gradually brought his two siblings on board, he's cooked up (quite literally) a reputation for excellence strongly linked to the promotion and sustainability of small producers. After all, he's well aware that producing excellence but not eating it doesn't help anybody and is a pointless exercise. "A gastronomic act is an agricultural act," is his belief. Anna too stresses the importance of "excellent relationships with suppliers" — who are named on the menu — and she's keen to underline the strong team of "*bravi*" they work with. Should you need further proof of Angelo's commitment to small artisan producers, then pay a visit to Milan's Mercato della Terra, the famous local farmers' market that he helped to found and that can draw thousands of people at the weekend.

Paolo explains that Angelo's dream was to establish a *grande classico*. And he's not the only one convinced that his brother has succeeded. L'Osteria del Treno is feted in restaurant guides and by its many visitors — regular or passing through. Yet Angelo laments the fact that it's no longer possible to describe himself as an *oste* on official forms rather than the general category of 'restaurateur'. "Technically I suppose I am, but have you ever thought about the form of the word 'osteria'?" he asks. "It's a marvellous combination of '*oste*' and '*storia*'. How wonderful is that?"

Pappardelle alle Verdure e Crema di Taleggio
Pappardelle with Vegetables and Taleggio Cream

A vegetable pasta with Taleggio. A predictable ingredient given Angelo's love and knowledge of cheese and the makers who supply the osteria.

SERVES 4

Pasta:

200g fine semolina

2 eggs

1 egg yolk

Salt

1 tsp olive oil

1 courgette, cut into batons

1 aubergine, cut into batons

1 pepper, cut into batons

Extra virgin olive oil

Salt, to taste

150g Taleggio

1 small glass of milk

Basil

Put the flour into a pile on a worktop, add the eggs and yolk, the salt, a trickle of oil, mix and knead thoroughly. Wrap in cling film and leave to rest for 30 minutes in the fridge.

Roll out the pasta into thin sheets. Cut large strips of about 2.5cm wide and 18cm long to form the pappardelle.

Wash and cut the vegetables into sticks. Cook each vegetable separately in a pan with extra virgin olive oil so that they remain crunchy. Adjust the seasoning.

Remove the crust from the Taleggio, cut into pieces and melt in a heat resistant bowl over a pan of boiling water with the addition of a drop of milk. Add enough milk to make a loose sauce but be careful not to make it too runny.

Cook the pappardelle in plenty of salted water, drain and mix with the vegetables, the Taleggio cream and basil.

Wine suggestion: Red – Valpolicella Superiore, Marion (Corvina, Corvinone blend)

Ossobuco alla Milanese
Braised Veal Shanks

One of Milan's best known recipes and very easy to cook at home. From the shin, osso means bone and buco, hole. Try to find ossibuchi which are the same size so that they all cook equally. Anna explains that "it's traditional to serve this tasty dish with a Milanese (saffron) risotto, polenta or with mashed potato."

SERVES 4

50g butter	Salt and pepper, to taste
2-3 tbsp olive oil	500ml meat stock
1 onion, finely chopped	1 bunch parsley, finely chopped
1 carrot, finely chopped	1 clove of garlic, finely chopped
4 veal ossibuchi, about 350g each	Lemon zest, grated
50g flour	Saffron risotto, polenta, or mashed potato, to serve
200ml white wine	

In a large pan put the butter and oil, add the onion and carrot and leave them to cook on a gentle heat. In the meantime prepare the *ossibuchi* by cutting the membrane that surrounds them with scissors. This will prevent them from expanding and twisting during cooking. Lightly coat them with flour.

When the onion and carrot are half cooked (about 15 minutes), add the *ossibuchi* to the pan and brown them well on all sides. Then add the white wine. Leave it to almost evaporate, season with salt and pepper, and then add the stock.

Cook on a low heat for at least an hour and a half, covering with a lid but leaving space for the air to escape. Give the pan a little shake from time to time, to avoid the *ossibuchi* sticking and add extra stock when necessary.

In the meantime, prepare the famous gremolada (or gremolata) by mixing the parsley, garlic and lemon zest, then adding to the pan 5 minutes before the end of cooking. Serve with your choice of saffron risotto, polenta or mashed potato.

Wine suggestion: Red – Ribolla Nera, Vigna Petrussa (Ribolla Nera)

Ratanà
Cesare Battisti

via De Castillia, 28
20124 Milan
T: +39 02 8712 8855
W: ratana.it

Opening hours: 12.30 -
14.30; 18.30 (*aperitivo*)
19.30 - 23.30
Closed: Mon and Tues in
winter; Sat and Sun from
15 Jun – 30 Sep
Holidays: 1 week in Jan and
2 weeks in Aug

Local folklore has it that the Priest of Ratanà, Don Giuseppe Gervasini, was a miracle worker. He lived at the end of the road where Cesare Battisti's restaurant is situated — hence the name.

So is Cesare religious? No, but he believes in sustaining the character of his area of Milan — though not nearly as strongly as he believes in true Milanese cooking. He's lost count of the fine dining chefs he's met who boasted of representing his hometown yet featured black cod on their menus. "These things don't belong here. It's better to extol what is ours," he says, adding that when he went market shopping with his mother as a youngster, "we'd buy eels and trout from the lakes but we never had sea bass."

It's not clear if Cesare had *rubitt* (Milanese dialect for small things) back then, but he does now. These are served at *aperitivi* time, and he likes their similarity to tapas. No carby, bready fillers here (although the grissini are noteworthy); rather small samples from the usual menu.

He applauds the virtues of regional cooking in Italy but questions the emphasis on complicated dishes stunningly presented. He won't play that game, stating almost defiantly, "The more fussy the Michelin-starred guys get, the simpler we make it."

Not that Ratanà is style-free. Far from it. The interior handsomely belies the building's former life as a railway depot. But then creative flair helps when you're refashioning rail ironware into sleek-looking tables and box shelving that's functionally fitting in more ways than one. In fact, look more closely

and you may recognise the origins of the water glasses. Yes, they're made from wine bottles, "by a friend of mine," says Cesare.

The restaurant is a magnet not just for groups of friends but for colleagues who flock here after work. Hence there may be creative industry punters wearing artfully distressed leather jackets and high-flyers in immaculately pressed tailor-made suits. Cesare explains that "lots of the senior businessmen in Milan come here to eat because they can relax after a day at work — and they can eat Lombard food." Which of course includes risotto — and Cesare's risotti are up there with the very best.

Cesare explains that the basis of the word 'ristorante' in Italian is 'ristorare', to restore and revive, so he feels duty bound to do just that. He seems to be succeeding. Outside on the garden terrace on a summer evening, it's impossible not to unwind. Young parents keep a distant yet watchful eye on their kids playing on the climbing frames, while kicking off their work shoes (literally) on to the wooden deck with its simple and very Italian-looking furniture beneath large white parasols, and taking a deep breath.

Looking after children is important at Ratanà. When the weather's wintry and playing outside isn't an option, then a large table inside is sacrificed at Sunday lunch for paper and pencils. "It's important to make sure kids are happy if you want parents to feel relaxed," says Cesare.

And it's those details that tell you the instant you walk in that people here know what they're doing. The staff are a good team and Cesare's a generous

boss. If you've worked well for him, and you want to go to get some experience elsewhere in the world, he'll phone his contacts to get it sorted.

He's even loosened up the staff attire. When he opened, the serving staff wore long, thin black ties and to-the-floor aprons. These days they wear brightly coloured, humorous house t-shirts. Maybe one with a graphic summary of *cassoeula*, a Milanese winter dish made with pig ears, skin and feet, or perhaps the Ratanà version of the famous Beatles' song, aka 'Luccio in the Sky with Diamonds — the freshwater fish compilation', *luccio* being pike.

But then it seems a fun place to work as well as to eat. If you want to sneak a peak into the kitchen, take a seat at the bar rather than a table. You get to chat to people serving and may even hear about the Priest of Ratanà; if you're able to answer two easy questions on him, you'll receive a discount.

So did he really perform miracles? Who knows? Still, he's sure to be thrilled that abandoned railway material has been so magically transformed in his name.

Mondeghili
Mondeghili

This is a classic Milanese dish and a good way of not wasting the meat used for making a good stock – essential in places that take risotto preparation seriously. Cesare serves his mondeghili in stylish paper cones and they're a great accompaniment to a glass of fizz while choosing from the menu.

SERVES 4-6

400g veal/beef (any cheap cut), cut into large pieces

½ clove of garlic

1 carrot, quartered

1 onion, quartered

100g stale bread soaked in milk

1 egg, beaten

20g Grana Padano, grated

Nutmeg, grated

Salt and pepper

Breadcrumbs, for coating

Extra virgin olive oil

Put the meat, garlic and vegetables into a large pan and cover with water. Make a stock by cooking on a low heat until the meat is cooked. (Probably a couple of hours depending on the cut and size of your meat).

Save the stock for general use and pass the meat, vegetables and softened bread through a mincer.

Mix in the egg, cheese, nutmeg, salt and pepper. Check the seasoning. Make small balls, the size of a large walnut and cover in breadcrumbs. Brown in a pan in a small amount of extra virgin olive oil or deep fry if you prefer. Serve while hot.

Wine suggestion: White sparkling – Nature Ecru Oltrepò Pavese Metodo Classico Extra Brut, Anteo (Pinot Nero)

Trota dell'Adamello Marinata, Arance Tarocco e Finocchietto Selvatico
Marinated Trout, Tarocco Blood Orange and Wild Fennel

Cesare buys his trout from a supplier who regularly sends him a quarterly water analysis and full progress report on the fish. His river trout are very big and he uses one of about 1.5 kg for this. When available, he uses Tarocco blood oranges but it's also a popular dish when other good quality oranges are used instead.

SERVES 4

2 x 350g trout	**Salad leaves**
25g salt	**Handful of wild fennel fronds**
55g sugar	**Extra virgin olive oil, to taste**
4 Tarocco blood oranges (if available)	

Fillet the trout and remove all bones. Mix the salt and sugar together and sprinkle evenly over the four fillets. Leave to rest in a non-reactive dish in the fridge for 6-8 hours with a weight on top.

Remove from the fridge, drain away any liquid and wipe the fillets clean with kitchen towel. Slice thinly and leave to rest in the juice of two oranges for 30 minutes.

Cut segments from the remaining oranges and serve the trout on top of salad leaves with the orange, a few torn wild fennel fronds and extra virgin olive oil.

Wine suggestion: White – Derthona, Vigneti Massa (Timorasso)

Montecalvo Versiggia/Oltrepò Pavese

There are many small villages and hamlets in the Oltrepò (which means 'beyond the Po River') Pavese of which Montecalvo Versiggia is one. The area is known for its *salumi* (Cacciatorino, Salame di Varzi and Coppa), apples, peaches, Voghera peppers, the Siras and Nisso di Menconico cheeses and its Pinot Nero.

If that isn't enough to start a party, the Oltrepò Pavese is also home to Stradella, of accordion-making fame. Or, the nearby provincial capital Pavia, as well as the town of Vigevano are both worth a visit.

Prato Gaio
Giorgio Liberti and Daniela Calvi

Frazione Versa, 16
27047 Montecalvo
Versiggia
T: +39 0385 99726
W: ristorantepratogaio.it

Opening hours: 12.30 –
14.00; 19.30 – 21.30
(times of last orders)
Closed: Mon and Tues
Holidays: early Jan
until shortly before
Valentine's Day

Giorgio Liberti, owner of the Prato Gaio restaurant, explains that he won't compromise on quality or cost. "I'd never have been a good accountant," he says. Which is interesting given that he qualified as one. But then so did Daniela Calvi, his head chef. So what happened? "It was fate," exclaims Giorgio.

These days he's more of an art and literature fan. He enjoys reading Artusi, old and contemporary recipe books, and listening to music. You'll hear gentle jazz in the restaurant, "or," as he puts it, "something that makes you dream. Background music shouldn't make you want to sing or dance."

How things have changed. Music in this area was once much less soothing. In fact, still visible behind the restaurant is the original *prato gaio*, the grassy area which was an open dance floor up until the end of the 1950s.

Giorgio took over the family business back in 1990, at the same time as Daniela Calvi joined. Daniela, who gave up accountancy when she got married and had a family, was living nearby when she heard that Giorgio's mother was looking for someone to help out generally and make pastries (her interest in cooking had started at school with desserts). From there, she learnt pastas, then antipasti and so on. Today she is managing the whole professional kitchen.

She has an uncommonly expressive face and admits she has a bit of a temper ("I'm precise and I don't like things being disorganised," she insists), but she runs a cheerful kitchen with lots of laughter despite the stresses and strains of keeping so many hungry diners happy.

Opposite top: The Prato Gaio restaurant

Bottom left: Giorgio Liberti

Giorgio has different skills. In fact he's the first to admit that he's not manually gifted. "I didn't learn to tie my shoelaces until I was 10 or 11," he says. But he's good at research. In fact he refuses to try food without knowing its provenance and history. He can expertly talk you through the different breads in the house basket: he suggests the Micca di Stradella or *Miccone* for the *salumi* he serves, or you could try the incredibly light grissini, which go well with *pancetta rotolata*.

However, as interested as Giorgio is in all foods from his *territorio*, he's especially enthusiastic about the wines; the restaurant list is a treasure trove of reasonably priced bottles of Buttafuoco, Bonarda and local Rieslings.

Giorgio believes that hunger is not just about a rumbling stomach "but also about culture." Which is why the menu used to be delivered verbally. However, as Giorgio insisted on telling the story behind every item, it took a long time. So the Prato Gaio menu is now printed — on beautiful thick paper with a seasonal picture of the Oltrepò Pavese and extracts from the writings of Mario Soldati and Gioacchino Rossini.

As well versed as he is in Oltrepò Pavese customs, his view is that "tradition is nothing other than successful innovation" ("*la tradizione non é altro che un innovazione ben riuscita*"). In other words if something works, it is accepted and eventually — after a few generations — it becomes traditional.

Giorgio never embraced accountancy. In fact, he hasn't fully embraced modern life (he refuses to use a computer). He's clearly much better suited to running a restaurant and promoting his *territorio* than auditing or double-entry bookkeeping.

Agnolotti di Stufato di Manzo al Sugo di Stufato
Beef-filled Agnolotti with a Beef Sauce

Daniela's servings – like her - are generous. Although this takes some time, it's a satisfying way to spend a few hours in the kitchen.

SERVES 6-8

Sauce:

100ml extra virgin olive oil

100g butter

100g onion, coarsely chopped

50g celery, coarsely chopped

Sprig of rosemary, chopped

50g pancetta, cubed

1kg beef braising steak, halved

150ml red wine, such as Bonarda
    dell'Oltrepò Pavese

2 bay leaves

Salt

Pinch each of ground nutmeg,
    cinnamon and black pepper

750ml meat stock

1 tbsp breadcrumbs

150g Parmesan, grated and extra for
    serving

1 egg, beaten

Pasta:

500g 00 flour

4 eggs

1 tbsp olive oil

In a large pan, heat the oil and butter and fry the onion, celery, rosemary and pancetta. Brown the beef on all sides. Add the wine, bay leaves, salt, spices and meat stock, cover and cook on a low heat for about 2 hours. Remove the lid and cook for a further hour.

Make the pasta by mixing the flour, eggs and oil to a smooth dough. Cover with cling film and leave to rest for about half an hour.

Remove the meat from the pan and chop it coarsely. Strain the cooking liquid, to separate the liquid from the vegetables, keeping both. In a blender, blitz the vegetables and just under half the meat to a rough paste, and add some of the cooking liquid to loosen. This will form the pasta filling, so season to taste and add the breadcrumbs, Parmesan and egg.

Roll out the pasta and place piles of filling the size of a small walnut, along one length. Fold over the pasta and press out round shapes with a pasta cutter, or cut with a knife and seal shut with a fork.

Cook in plenty of salted water and serve with the remaining meat heated through adding some cooking liquid if needed. Finish with grated Parmesan.

Wine suggestion: Red – a Bonarda from the Oltrepò Pavese

Salame di Cioccolato con Biscotti Secchi, Albicocche Candite e Pistacchi
Chocolate Salame with Biscuits, Dried Apricots and Pistachios

This is a rich dessert which Daniela likes to serve with pistachio ice cream, or berries if available.

SERVES 12

250g dark chocolate
  (70% cocoa solids)

150g butter

1 espresso cup of coffee

4 egg yolks

4 tbsp caster sugar

300g dry biscuits, broken into
  small pieces

100g pistachios, coarsely chopped

100g dried apricots, chopped

Icing sugar

Fruit, for decorating

Pistachio ice cream, to serve
  (optional)

Break up the chocolate and melt it in a heatproof bowl suspended over a pan of simmering water, but not touching the water. Remove from the heat, add the butter and mix it in with a spatula until it's completely melted and you have a creamy mixture. Add the coffee and leave it at room temperature to cool down.

Separately, in a large mixing bowl, whisk the egg yolks with the sugar to obtain an airy and frothy mixture. Incorporate the melted chocolate and mix well. Finally mix in the broken biscuits, the pistachios and the chopped apricots. Leave to rest for a few minutes in the fridge to slightly harden the mixture.

Work the mixture with your hands to form a salame shape. Wrap it in greaseproof paper, twisting both ends closed like a sweet. Leave it to set in the fridge for 4-5 hours.

Cut the salame into regular slices and serve with a shaking of icing sugar and decorate the plate with fruit. Serve with a scoop of pistachio ice cream (if using).

Wine suggestion: Red dessert wine – Sangue di Giuda dell'Oltrepò Pavese DOC (Croatina, Barbera, Uva Rara, Ughetta, Pinot Nero).

Monte Isola

The biggest lake island in Italy, Monte Isola on Lake Iseo is accessible by a regular ferry service from the mainland. It's worth doing the short crossing even if just for a wander and a coffee on the island. There's more to see for those who wish to explore.

Fishermen on other lakes of Lombardy will tell you that the best fishing nets (and some good sports nets too) are made on Monte Isola because "they double knot the nets so they don't slip and change shape".

For such a small place, it has a big name in gastronomy, boasting its own highly regarded *sardine essicate*, salami and olive oil.

Locanda al Lago
Stefania Soardi

Località Carzano, 38
25050 Monte Isola
T: +39 030 988 6472
W: locandaallago.it

Opening hours: 12.30 –
14.30; 19.30 – 22.30
Closed: Tues from
mid-Sep to May; then open
every day
Holidays: 7 Jan until the
last weekend of Feb

Crossing Lake Iseo by ferry from Sale Marasino to Carzano on Monte Isola on the way to Locanda al Lago is a magical pre-antipasto. The ferry crew are fun and the five-minute sail puts everything in context. At least it does if you choose to eat fish. And of course you should. A few meat dishes appear on the menu as a sort of token gesture but, really, why would you?

Stefania Soardi, who runs Locanda al Lago, comes from a fishing family. In Slow Food circles, her father Fernando is a bit of a star as he successfully campaigned to have the lake's *sardina essicata* awarded a Presidium. He started professional life as an accountant but was unable to resist the call of his beloved Lake Iseo. In 1984, to his mother's dismay, he announced that he was leaving his office desk for a boat and life as a professional fisherman.

It's a similar story with Stefania's brother, Andrea, who worked in IT before realising that a life on the water would be so much more appealing than one in front of a computer. He now looks after the family business, which is run alongside the restaurant. He produces the *sardine essicate* (which are, confusingly, not sardines). These fish are either dried whole by hanging up on large racks or filleted and laid flat in which case, says Andrea, laughing, "we turn them a couple of times a day like Champagne. But we don't have a machine; we do it all by hand."

He uses Sale di Cervia as a conserving salt because of its regular-shaped grains, and when there's no one keeping an eye on the fish, they're covered by nets to protect them from the birds. He's proud to emphasise the fact that the *sardine* that they dry "don't come from Lake Garda. They're ours — from Lake Iseo."

When not supervising the drying of fish, Andrea descales and fillets whatever the restaurant needs from the latest catch and produces jars of fish fillets in oil and bottarga, which features on Locanda al Lago's menu in a risotto of lake fish. This joint activity is a big advantage for a fish restaurant that doesn't precook and has no freezer; either Stefania or Andrea can always use whatever fish is caught, so nothing goes to waste.

Although Stefania has never professionally caught fish, she didn't have a direct route to the restaurant either, coming from a public relations background. Still, as she rather charmingly puts it, "Perhaps when you're born into a business you can't help but fall in love with it." Of course, given that the restaurant was first opened in 1948 by her grandmother, it's certainly a family business. It was closed from 1998 to 2005, but was then revamped and reopened by Stefania's parents.

Stefania talks about a late 1950s film she's seen in which her young father is helping her grandmothers to unload wine from a boat a short way up from where the restaurant is. Very little has changed — there are still silk prints on the walls that were in the original restaurant — although the terrace that juts out over the water is a relatively recent addition. And a welcome one. It's indisputably a joyful place to sit and eat while watching the boats, the sunshine on the water and perhaps even a duck walking up the terrace steps, occasionally leaving an egg behind. It's an especially good place to enjoy a glass of *bollicine*. "Franciacorta's next door and fizz is a great match for our food," Stefania explains.

She's the first to admit that the cooking here is simple but, as she points out, "there's no need to complicate things because we use top quality ingredients." The longstanding regulars certainly know it. When her father calls to tell them what he's caught, they soon turn up in eager anticipation.

You can't get a fish dinner much fresher — or more local. And you certainly can't get a better post-*digestivo* than returning to the mainland across the lake. The reflections of twinkling lights and the breeze from the water on your face are an enchanting finale.

Zuppa di Pesce al Lago
Lake Fish Soup

This soup is a very light broth with the pieces of fish cooked briefly so that they don't break up. Obviously, at Locanda al Lago they use fish from the lake, avoiding species such as trout which they consider to be too fatty for the initial stock. Gamberi di lago are added when available.

SERVES 4-5

2 tbsp olive oil, plus extra for drizzling

2 small onions, coarsely chopped

4 small carrots, coarsely chopped

2 sticks of celery, coarsely chopped

1 glass of white wine

4 litres water

800g canned tomatoes

Fish bones and trimmings for stock

Salt and pepper

500g of varied fish fillets, cut into small pieces

Salt and pepper

12-15 small slices of bread

Oregano, finely chopped

Handful of parsley, chopped

Heat the olive oil in a large saucepan and fry the chopped vegetables gently until softened. Add the wine, water and canned tomatoes to the pan along with whatever fish trimmings you are using. Bring to the boil and then leave uncovered on a medium simmer until reduced by half – between 1-2 hours.

Take a large mesh sieve or colander and drain the liquid into another pan and then drain again through a fine sieve. (Stefania insists that it's quicker done in this way.) Leave it to rest for an hour or so, in order that the "flavours make friends."

Reheat the broth and adjust the seasoning. Add the selected pieces of fish and cook for 1-2 minutes so that they stay whole.

Toast the bread, drizzle with oil and sprinkle over the oregano. Serve the soup sprinkled with parsley with slices of toast.

Wine suggestion: Sparkling white – Alma Cuvée Brut Franciacorta, Bellavista (Chardonnay, Pinot Nero, Pinot Bianco)

La Millefoglie di Sardine con Chips di Polenta
Fish and Crispy Polenta Millefeuille

These are made at Locanda al Lago with the island's sardine essicate, dried fish. Home dry your fish should you wish, or use fresh sardines or mackerel.

SERVES 4

100g polenta

6 small fish fillets, cut into pieces

1 tbsp olive oil for frying

3 tbsp white wine vinegar

Handful of chopped parsley

Extra virgin olive oil, to taste

Pre-heat the oven to 200°C.

Cook the polenta according to the pack instructions, keeping it slightly looser than usual and season it well. Put it onto a large, or two small non-stick baking sheets and spread out very thinly with a palette knife. Don't grease the sheets, because the polenta won't stay in place if you do. Place in the oven for 10 minutes. Turn the oven down to 160°C and release the polenta sheet with the palette knife (it may stick in places so ease it away gently). Turn the polenta sheet over and return to the oven for about 15 minutes, turning it over every 3-4 minutes until it's completely dry. Leave to cool and then break into pieces.

Heat the oil in a non-stick pan and cook the fish pieces over a medium heat for a few minutes until lightly golden on both sides. Remove the fish from the pan and leave to one side. Heat the vinegar and parsley in the pan for 30-40 seconds then leave to cool and add olive oil to taste.

Heat the polenta in a 160°C oven before serving (if you'd like it warm), then alternate layers of polenta and fish, then season with the dressing.

Wine suggestion: Sparkling white – Dosage Zero Millesimato or Satèn Millesimato, Ca' del Bosco (Chardonnay, Pinot Nero, Pinot Bianco; Chardonnay, Pinot Bianco)

Morbegno

The crisp, clean air of Morbegno tells you it's a mountain town. It also feels like a hard-working, not late-night-partying place but there are some decent bars, and a couple of elegant churches.

Well situated for visiting the Valle del Bitto and the Valchiavenna, it's rather conveniently just down the road from Sondrio should you wish to spend time (but not stay overnight) in the provincial capital.

Osteria dal Crotto
Maurizio Vaninetti

via Pedemontana, 22
23017 Morbegno
T: +39 0342 614 800
W: osteriadelcrotto.it

Opening hours: 12.30 –
14.30; 19.30 – 22.30
Closed: Sun evening and
Mon lunchtime
Holidays: 2 weeks between
Aug and Sep

The name of Maurizio Vaninetti's osteria makes sense once you know that there's a grotto, or *crotto* in the kitchen. At a steady temperature of 5-6°C, he uses it to keep drinks cool when the fridge is full.

Although it's on the edge of central Morbegno, the osteria feels as though it's in the middle of nature. The outside terrace with a view over the rooftops and campanile is backed by a large plant-covered stone wall, which is so cold that on a hot summer's night it feels like nature's air conditioning.

But clearing the three metre-high plants from the terrace when he arrived to set up his osteria was one of the easier problems Maurizio had to solve. More of a challenge was that, having worked in a fabrics factory, he only had limited restaurant experience from helping out friends. You might even argue that he took a courageous decision to leave steady work to start up his own business in an area he knew very little about (his wife, he says, felt it was more stupid than brave, but then she's in charge of the books).

But whatever experience and knowledge he may have lacked, he did know plenty of people who were willing to help him. So after a research trip in which he saw a lot of "self-important and conceited cooking", as he describes it, he returned home to the obvious treasures of his *territorio*. All he needed to do next was discover the best producers.

His contacts generously opened their address books to him so that he quickly moved, he says, "from international cooking to produce-led cooking." He then went even further. Using indigenous grains and local foods "at the prime moment" was what made him happiest, so in 2003, he

decided that he'd only use produce from his *territorio*. Whereas before he'd occasionally buy lamb from Scotland or New Zealand, from that point he's only bought locally raised meat. Even his cheese board no longer includes cheeses from France (which, let's face it, isn't too far away). Now they're all local, including a vertical selection of Bitto Storico from just down the road in Gerola Alta.

And, in the spring and summer, Teresina, who works front of house, goes up around Morbegno or Gerola on her day off to forage for wild herbs, which are used in a range of dishes that have got people talking. In fact, some diners come just for those.

But even more come for the wide range of specialities such as *violino di capra* or *filetto di lavarello del Lago di Como*. As well as Slow Food presidia: *formaggio Valli del Bitto*, *grano saraceno di Teglio* and *Stracchino all'antica delle Valli Orobiche*.

And the wine list has evolved in keeping with the menu changes. Now, 90 per cent of what Maurizio sells is from the Valtellina, We'll let him have the other 10 per cent for the pinot noirs ("my little passion"). He's especially

interested in organic and natural wines, and delighted about the number of young and dynamic producers in the Valtellina.

And he's excited that people from far away are now interested in his area's wines and artisan foods, although he has reservations about developing a big export market, instead hoping that people will travel to taste and experience the specialities in situ. "I should go to England to eat a great Stilton," he explains. "I don't think I can appreciate it properly if it's gone for a walk for six months." Which is why he feels that coming here to eat bresaola is best: because "it's part of the whole: the air, the people and the mountains."

As for food in the future, he's convinced that people will be more interested in local producers. "Those of us in the Valtellina are very proud of our wines and our products here," he says. "I don't want to move elsewhere. I like that there's a micro-economy around my restaurant — and that people bring me surplus carrots from their gardens."

Formaggio di Capra con Insalata di Orto
Goat's Cheese with Garden Salad

Maurizio works closely with lots of dedicated local producers and knows that often the best way of presenting their goods is to serve them simply. Here he combines a creamy but full-flavoured goat's cheese with cured goat meat, violino di capra.

SERVES 4

Small handful of parsley, very finely chopped

150g soft goat's cheese, at room temperature

180g cured goat's meat or other local cured meat, sliced

4 small handfuls of fresh salad leaves

Extra virgin olive oil

Mix the finely chopped parsley with the cheese. Divide the meat and cheese evenly between four plates. Wash and dry the salad leaves, divide those equally and dress each plate with the olive oil.

Wine suggestion: White – Ronco Valene, Fay (Sauvignon, Incrocio Manzoni)

Farfalle di Segale con Ragù di Capriolo
Farfalle with Venison Ragù

Maurizio sometimes makes his own farfalle with a mix of wheat and buckwheat flour, but dried pasta is always an option. He finishes this off in the oven, but for the small quantity used here, it's easier to keep it on the hob and ensure it doesn't dry out.

SERVES 4

200g venison (roe deer), chopped to a coarse mince

Olive oil, for frying

100g each of carrot, celery, onion, chopped

Small handful of dried porcini, soaked and finely chopped

100ml red wine

A few juniper berries

1 cinnamon stick

A few cloves

A splash of brandy

Small amount of meat stock

320g dried farfalle

Butter and grated Parmesan, to taste

Brown the meat in the heated oil. Add the chopped vegetables, mushrooms and the wine, then the juniper, cinnamon and cloves, the brandy and enough meat stock to almost cover. Keep covered on a gentle heat until the meat is cooked through and the flavours have amalgamated, adding further stock if required.

Cook the pasta in plenty of salted water until not quite done. Drain and sauté with the meat sauce. Add fresh butter and Parmesan to taste.

Wine suggestion: Red – Sassela, Sassi Solivi, Cooperativa Agricola Triasso e Sassella (Nebbiolo)

Fratelli Ciapponi
Primo and Dario Ciapponi

Piazza 3 Novembre, 23
23017 Morbegno
T: +39 0342 610 223
W: ciapponi.com

Opening hours: 08.30 –
12.30; 15.30 – 19.00
Closed: Sun, and Mon
afternoon

You could call Fratelli Ciapponi a food shop, but that gives no idea of how intriguing and evocative it is. Owned and run by the Ciapponi family for generations, it's how we like to imagine shopping once was.

Outside the shop sits the bike that Primo Ciapponi once used for making deliveries. It's been a while since he's cycled — but then he was born in 1924. It's also a while since he and his younger brother Dario spent six hours climbing uphill to reach the Alpeggi pastures for Bitto cheese. That cheese, however, is still a big part of the shop, helped by the cellar which provides ideal conditions for storing Bitto Storico.

It was back in 1905 that Pietro, their great grandfather, started to store Bitto. He'd buy the wheels directly from the producers and 'sign contracts' with a handshake; indeed both Dario and Primo still have very firm grips. The cheeses are still turned weekly, and cleaned fortnightly, and two or three whole wheels are sold every week. There's a separate room where you can choose from different maturities of Bitto Storico as well as other excellent cheeses, locally produced bresaola, and salumi, including horse and goat.

Wandering around Fratelli Ciapponi is a truly delightful and educational experience, revealing many other treasures that are not for sale: its first till, which is over 100 years old, various scales, meat slicers and intriguing tools. People also travel from far and wide to source top quality Valtellina specialities — and to get advice on them. And locals frequently use the attractive frontage as a backdrop for wedding photos.

It's not immediately obvious how large the shop is, but there are numerous rooms at the rear, and the steps in the wine room (beneath an archway with 1692 on it) lead down to a sizeable wine cellar.

The shopping experience here is as far removed from impersonal supermarket spending as you can imagine. "Stock control is done in our heads" explains Paolo, Dario's son.

Paolo has taken over with his cousin Alberto, but Primo and Dario are still active. They come downstairs from their homes above the shop every day to talk to customers. A food shop? Yes, and so, so much more.

Opposite from top: the brothers chatting outside the shop; Primo Ciapponi; Dario Ciapponi

Mortara

At the centre of Lomellina, Mortara is considered the *oca*, or goose, capital of Lombardy, and indeed of Italy.

Throughout the town there are foods on sale featuring various types of goose meat or fat, including bread which is only made in the winter, and sweet biscuits. There's also a goose festival, the Sagra del Salame d'Oca di Mortara.

When you've had your fill of goose meat, there are some interesting churches, most notably the Basilica of San Lorenzo and the imposing Chiesa Santa Croce.

Trattoria Guallina
Elena Delù

via Molino Faenza, 19
Guallina
27036 Mortara
T: +39 0384 91962
W: trattoriaguallina.it

Opening hours: 12.30 –
14.00; 20.00 – 22.00
Closed: Tues
Holidays: mid-Jun until
early Jul

As you drive the short distance from Mortara's town centre to the hamlet of Guallina, Elena Delù's trattoria and its red sign with a white goose stand like a culinary beacon ahead of you. But the emblematic logo announces more than the restaurant. This is Lombardy's goose heartland.

Don't think, however, that you'll always be able to pick and choose from a menu of goose dishes. You certainly will in the winter months, as that's the right time for eating goose meat, explains Elena. Even though she's able to buy it throughout the year, she observes the seasonal conventions, so at Trattoria Guallina, it's a winter meat. People come from all over Italy — 'goose tourists' as they're sometimes called — to eat it during the cold months. It's unsurprising that the most popular items on the menu are the risotto with goose salami and the goose breast.

But the restaurant doesn't just use one single product; there's a bounty of renowned produce in this area. In spring the menu features asparagus, particularly the *asparago di Cilavegna*, while in summer there's a move towards duck dishes, and in autumn mushrooms are more prominent. And of course there's great excitement in June when the sweet red onions from nearby Breme arrive.

Nevertheless, throughout the year there's a tempting selection of goose salumi on the antipasto menu. Perhaps a galantina with goose, pistachio and black truffle or *prosciutto d'oca stagionato*.

Elena's keen to keep the traditional products going, although she admits that many of the classic goose dishes have been lightened up from their rich and heavy preparation methods 50 years ago.

Above left: Elena Delù

She's not just a fan of goose meat and all the other local specialities — she's pretty knowledgeable on them too. She'll explain, for example, that the goose ravioli are made with roasted thighs and why spinach works well with this dish.

She's also an accomplished team player, possibly because she used to be a serious sportswoman — volleyball was her sport of choice when younger. That sense of team work means that there's an amiable efficiency between front of house and the kitchen staff. It also helps that Elena's husband is a chef, so she understands the culture.

The current chef at Trattoria Guallina is Carlo Carrega who grew up in a family of professional cooks and restaurateurs. He says that he's learnt a lot here about using the local *borlotti di Gambolò*, and of course cooking goose. He even makes — very good — bread with the locally popular *ciccioli d'oca*,

which he describes simply as "the goose skin, cut up and cooked in goose fat."

And of course, even outside of the winter months, you can't escape the importance of geese in this area and in this restaurant — even if you drive to it from Vigevano rather than through Mortara. There's a large picture on the dining room wall, which shows the Lomellina with its winding roads, fields and poplars, and naturally a family of geese. This and the red sign certainly show you where you are — but the Guallina food expresses the fact most eloquently of all.

Misto di Salumi
Mixed Cured Meats

Although most "goose tourists" know to come in the winter, even people who are passing through in the summer are keen to try the famous local speciality. Elena serves a generous antipasto mix of cured meats to solve this problem.

Galantina d'oca (a mix of goose meat and pork with pistachios)

Mortadellina d'oca di Mortara (pork and goose liver)

Petto d'oca stagionato (matured goose meat, two months)

Salame d'oca di Mortara IGP

An assortment of breads

Make sure that the cured meats are at room temperature at the time of serving. Elena always ensures that there's a variety of excellent breads to accompany these containing different flours and seeds and some grissini for textural contrast.

Wine suggestion: Sparkling rosé – Roccapietra Cruasé, Scuropasso (Pinot Nero)

Risotto con gli Asparagi
Asparagus Risotto

They don't just enjoy the white and pink asparago de Cilavegna from the Lomellina in Mortara. This risotto recipe works well with any asparagus spears.

SERVES 2

100g butter

2 generous tbsp extra virgin olive oil

½ white onion, finely chopped

8 asparagus spears cut into fine rounds – retain the tips for garnish

500ml meat stock

160g Carnaroli rice

125ml white wine

Salt and pepper

2 handfuls of grated Grana Padano

2 cloves of garlic, finely chopped

A few sprigs of parsley, finely chopped

In a pan, melt 50g of the butter gently with the oil. Add the onion and asparagus rounds and cook gently over a low heat for 5 minutes. Keep the meat stock gently simmering in a separate pan.

Add the rice to the first pan with the asparagus and coat thoroughly in the oil. Add the white wine and when it's nearly absorbed, add enough meat stock to just cover the rice. When it returns to the boil add salt and pepper. Add the stock slowly, spoonful by spoonful and keep stirring.

About 9 minutes from adding the salt and pepper, add the grated Grana Padano and continue to spoon in the stock until the rice is cooked. Add the garlic and parsley and mix in the remaining 50g of butter to make it creamy. Cook the remaining spears in salted water. Serve the risotto garnished with the spears.

Wine suggestion: White – Camarà, Tenuta Mazzolino (Chardonnay)

Palazzolo sull'Oglio

The tall Torre del Popolo, the symbol of the city of Palazzolo, announces the town from beyond the Oglio river on which it sits and across which its (sloping) Roman bridge is found.

Known in the 19th century as 'little Manchester' because of its role as an industrial centre, it still has a certain energy about it. Especially when major football matches are being screened and the bars around Piazza Roma and Piazza Vincenza Rosa erect stacked seating to accommodate the enthusiastic audience.

Osteria della Villetta
Maurizio Rossi and Maria Grazia Omodei

via G Marconi 104
25036 Palazzolo sull'Oglio
T: +39 030 740 1899
W: osteriadellavilletta.it

Opening hours: 12.00 –
15.00; 19.30 – 24.00
Closed: all day Sun
and Mon; dinner on
Tues and Wed
Holidays: 1 week in Jan and
2 weeks in Aug

"Traditional cooking requires time," explains Maurizio Rossi, "so people eat things here that they don't have time to make at home. Things their grandmothers and mothers used to cook for them."

And it's traditional food that's the focus of the menu at Osteria della Villetta, housed in a striking mint-green villa a few small steps from the quiet local train station of Palazzolo sull'Oglio. The Rossi family have been working in this building since 1900, when they moved their original osteria from around the corner. Maurizio is the fourth generation to supervise the offering of good food, good wine — and good socialising.

Because it's not just about the food. The social side and community involvement has always been important. Back in the 1950s the osteria had the only television in the village. There's still an evocative photograph on the wall of people watching an early broadcast.

Maurizio took over from his father in 1989. When he was younger, he had only helped out a little, occasionally serving at tables or making coffees, as his parents were keen for him and his brother to study. Which they did but Maurizio couldn't resist the pull of a professional life in the osteria. Nor the attraction of the Slow Food movement, which he's supported from the very start.

His wife Grazia remembers those years fondly "because for us Slow Food went beyond the idea of what one eats. It was a big socially transformative project." It's not surprising that they were excited by these ideas as they'd met when both politically active — and very young. In those days, Grazia says, smiling, "I thought I'd change the world."

Opposite centre: Grazia

But away from the political campaigning, it was life as normal back in Palazzolo when Maurizio's mother told Grazia on first meeting her "he's the best looking, the most intelligent, the most *bravo*." "She thought quite highly of me," Maurizio grins.

As did Grazia. Marriage was next and a mere two months later life changed again when Maurizio took over the management of the osteria from his parents. Back then, Grazia taught children with learning difficulties. She went part-time when their son was born, and from that moment helped out in the osteria too.

When Maurizio's mother died, Grazia stepped into her head cook's shoes and took over the kitchen despite having no formal training. But having worked alongside Maurizio's mother she knew that no changes were needed. "We want to keep a culture of straightforward food that's at risk of disappearing. It's our ambition to pass on the baton — to preserve this way of cooking and socialising together," she explains.

Maurizio feels that "cooking should have deep roots. One shouldn't just improvise and make it up because improvised cooking doesn't have a history. Form should never overtake substance. A dish should never look better than it tastes."

But although it's a place that is unrepentantly attached to traditional recipes ("tripe, *bollito*, *polpette* and *stoccafisso* on Friday"), that doesn't mean that these haven't been fine-tuned. Nowadays vegetarians say that this is one of the few places that takes their choices seriously. The kitchen uses less butter than earlier generations and favours extra virgin olive oil from nearby Lake Iseo.

Above: Maurizio and Grazia

But unlike the dishes, praise for the food hasn't lightened in the slightest. Even the great chef Alain Ducasse declared, "The food you eat here tells you that you can be nowhere else." And Italy's near-deified culinary maestro Gualtiero Marchesi (a particularly big fan of the *polpette*) included the osteria in a list of his 11 favourite places to eat. In the world.

But the couple were already big fans of Marchesi's for another reason. "His food's very clean. There's never an imposition of tastes but a combination," as Maurizio puts it. And that's the problem he has with lots of today's chefs who, "overlap too many tastes so that you no longer know what you're eating."

It's not all tradition, however. Both Maurizio and Grazia are modern art enthusiasts. This interest is visible in the many drawings on the wall (some done on the paper place mats) by some greats of Italian modern art: Mimmo Rotella, Arnaldo Pomodoro and Valerio Adami among them.

Of course, old things are appreciated too; the interior of the osteria is substantially as it's been since Maurizio's parents' day. He knows that La Villetta has a certain magic. Not only is it full of soul, but of old curiosities: scales, an accordion, a meat slicer, an old chequers board, a fruit juice-

pressing machine from the 1950s and a *bollito misto* vessel from a large hotel in Torino from around 1890. It's a treasure trove.

Which may be why the designer Jasper Morrison chose the osteria as the place for the photo shoot of his new range of Alessi crockery. And Michelangelo Pistoletto, who Grazia believes is "not just an artist but a great intellectual," introduced a new project here.

The large mirror has been in place since the start — well over a century — but was important for more than just aesthetic reasons. Maurizio's father would sit at the back of the side room from where he could see the bar. And it enabled his grandmother to see what was happening in the kitchen from the main room. "An early security camera," says Maurizio.

These days Grazia doesn't need a mirror to know what people need. She has, it seems, eyes in the back of her head. She now runs the kitchen as if she's always worked there, keeping control with a smile. And she'll go out to tables to check that all is OK then glide to the till to take a payment. She's fast but organised and methodical, gracefully changing beat in time with the alternating rhythms of patience and urgency, of brigade encouragement and diner demand.

She also looks after their son, Jacopo, and is both intrigued and proud that he has "an amazing palate." He knows if the sausages have been made with different seasonings — but then sausages, rice and vegetables is his favourite meal. Like Maurizio's parents, Jacopo's are keen for him to "study and have his own experiences" before choosing whether he wants to work in the osteria or not. If he does, he's sure to be as efficient as his parents who have set a great example.

On a busy lunchtime, diners sit down and are quickly served a glass of their choice. Perhaps Franciacorta fizz from a mere 5km away. Given a beautiful plate of bread they either sit quietly relaxing after the morning's work or chat to their neighbours. There's an understanding that lots of people who come for lunch need to get out quickly and that others have more time to linger. No matter. All are made to feel welcome and eat as they wish. "We do a lot of business at lunchtime," says Maurizio. "Managers arrive angry, and after a couple of hours, they leave happy and calm again. People don't just come here to eat but to relax and put the brakes on the speed of everyday life."

Which sounds easy, but he understands that "the simple things are the hardest to do well." The couple must be succeeding. Marchesi defined La Villetta as "the quintessential osteria".

It's certainly like them: stimulating, fun — and unapologetically authentic. "There are lots of restaurants that want to seem like old osterie but they're not," says Maurizio. "La Villetta is 'un posto vero' and as real as it's always been."

Involtini di Verza
Savoy Cabbage Rolls

Grazia serves her involtini alongside a guanciale bollito with salsa verde and a beef patty, but they are substantial enough by themselves. Breadcrumbs are an important part of the filling so be sure to use good quality bread.

SERVES 4

200g cooked pork loin, chopped – not too finely

110g pork sausage, cooked and chopped – not too finely

80g matured Grana Padano, grated

55g breadcrumbs

1 small egg, beaten

Salt, pepper and grated nutmeg, to taste

300ml meat stock

8 Savoy cabbage leaves, or more depending on the size of your leaves

Olive oil

1 onion, finely chopped

50g pancetta, chopped

To make the filling, mix in a bowl the pork, sausage, Grana Padano, breadcrumbs, beaten egg and seasonings. The mixture shouldn't be too dry so add some meat stock if necessary.

Lightly blanche the cabbage leaves. Drain and spread them out on kitchen towel to dry. Divide the filling between the cabbage leaves, then roll them up and close like a package.

Heat a small amount of oil in a non-stick pan and lightly fry the onion and pancetta. Cover the bottom of the pan with heated meat stock and put the rolls to simmer gently for about 20 minutes, adding further stock if needed. Serve while warm.

Wine suggestion: Sparkling – Franciacorta Extra Brut DOCG, Ferghettina (Chardonnay, Pinot Nero)

Pesche Ripiene
Stuffed Peaches

Grazia uses "beautifully ripe peaches", but this recipe will enhance fruits
that are less than perfect.

SERVES 4

4 peaches

25g Amaretti biscuits, broken into
   fine crumbs

25g savoiardi biscuits or sponge
   fingers, broken into small crumbs

25g ground almonds

2 tbsp Marsala

Knob of butter

½ tbsp caster sugar

50ml water

Pre-heat the oven to 180°C.

Cut the peaches in half, remove the stones and place the halves cut side up in an oven dish.

In a bowl, mix together the biscuit crumbs and the almonds. Add the Marsala to form a paste. Fill each peach half with this mixture and put a small amount of butter on top of each one. Dissolve the sugar in the water and pour enough into the bottom of the baking dish so that it's thinly covered. Bake in the oven for 10 minutes.

Remove from the oven and add more sugar water if needed. Return to the oven for another 10 minutes. Remove the peaches from the oven, turn them upside down to remove their skins and serve with the cooking liquid.

Wine suggestion: Fortified wine – Pinodisé, Contadi Castaldi (Chardonnay)

Salò

The locals freely admit that Salò has a reputation for exclusivity, but then it does have large, expensive waterfront properties — partly due to the fact that, as the same locals like to point out, the sun shines on the west (their) side of the lake throughout the day, whereas on the opposite, eastern or Veronese side, the sun only shines in the morning.

Which is why all day long in the summer, the waterfront is busy with locals and visitors admiring the view, watching the boats, taking the sun and dangling their feet in the cooling water.

Osteria dell'Orologio
Alberto Giacomini and Sara Marini

via Butturini, 26
25087 Salò
T: +39 0365 290 158
W: osteriadellorologio
salo.com

Opening hours: 12.30 –
14.30; 19.30 – 22.30
Closed: Wed
Holidays: variable

"Alberto, a glass of my favourite fizz when you have a moment please." It's a gloriously sunny noon in Salò and the locals are arriving at Osteria dell' Orologio for their daily *aperitivo*. More than regulars, these are the men known as the '*calicisti*', who turn up every day for a glass, or *calice*, of wine. They're such a part of the osteria that their caricatures, drawn by Giancarlo Zucconelli — aka Zuc, a well-known cartoonist from Verona — are on display along the wall in the first room. The *calicisti* are proud of their cartoons and keen to point out their own — perhaps making you hazard a guess first. For a group of professionals — architects, doctors and entrepreneurs among them —they all seem to be born raconteurs.

Every day they gather at the wooden bar and take their pick from the lovingly compiled wine list and its constantly changing choice by the glass. Alberto, the owner, is a committed oenophile. He's particularly fond of Ca' del Bosco Franciacorta so there's a magnum chilled and ready to go in a big ice bucket. Early on in his relationship with Sara, his wife and colleague, he turned up at her house with a bottle of Ca' del Bosco Annamaria Clementi. "It was fantastic," she smiles, "and it's still my favourite wine." She also loves Champagne, but that's where Alberto couldn't accommodate her. This is an all-Italian wine list.

And an all-Italian, seasonal food menu. So expect lots of lake fish from May to September and hearty Lombard meats — perhaps *spiedo Bresciano* or guinea fowl — in the winter. There are no concessions here for the unadventurous tourist.

But then not many passing foreigners make it to Orologio. Several who have bought properties around the lake are regulars, but then they're in the

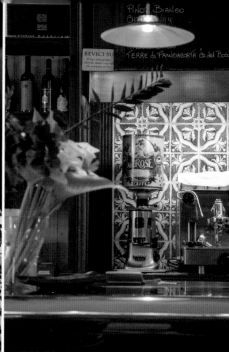

know. They also appreciate that a 100-year-old building with very thick walls will have no mobile reception. No matter. Alberto happily takes calls for regulars on the landline.

It's that sort of welcoming informality that also means there's no obligation to have a full meal — although temptation may be hard to resist if you see what's being served (or if you've been enticed by the daily specials on the blackboard outside).

And the kitchen makes a big effort to use everything. If you're lucky you'll be there on a day when rabbit's being cooked and a plate of *frattaglie* — leftover offal that is chopped into small pieces and fried with some rosemary — is handed out as bar nibbles. Or perhaps courgette flowers or fish *polpette* will be served with your drink.

Of course, there's more than just bar food here. As well as normal tables there's a very large one upstairs for groups or communal dining. But usually sole diners choose to eat at the bar downstairs where they can chat to Alberto when he isn't otherwise occupied, though even in the middle of a rush he's calm, and somehow all-welcoming and all-seeing. As is Sara, but then she used to run her own pizzeria in Gardone before joining forces with Alberto.

Opposite centre: Alberto Giacomoni

Above centre: Sara Marini

Opposite top: Some of the *calicisti*

Appropriately, given its name, there are lots of clocks around Osteria dell'Orologio. Not all of them are accurate, but the *calicisti* seem to know when it's time to head home. They gradually depart, still in a mood of lively bonhomie, perhaps planning their annual November trip with Alberto and fondly recollecting previous visits to Barcelona for paella, Puglia for wine and Brittany for oysters. Should any of them move away then a black band is put on their cartoon for six months before being replaced by a *calicisto* in waiting.

If you want a view over the lake while eating in Salò, then wander along the waterfront, and battle for an unencumbered view — at a premium of course. If you want good, straightforward seasonal food with a non-touristy vibe then walk along the via Butturini that runs parallel with the *lungolago*, and join the town's fun-loving locals in a glass of their favourite fizz.

Spaghetti con Coregone e Sarde
Lake Fish Spaghetti

Sitting on Lake Garda as it does, it's inevitable that Osteria dell'Orologio serves fresh lake fish – in this recipe local coregone and sarde with local capers and olives. So, follow in their footsteps and use fish that is easily available to you and provides a mix of flavours. They usually make their own egg pasta but, for the home cook, dried spaghetti is the more practical option.

SERVES 4

320g spaghetti

440g of two different types of fish, filleted, skinned and cut into small pieces

1 tbsp extra virgin olive oil

1 clove of garlic, finely chopped

400g cherry tomatoes (around 28 in total), halved

10g capers

10g olives

A few basil leaves

Cook the pasta in plenty of salted boiling water. Sauté the fish in the oil and garlic for a few minutes and then add the tomatoes, capers and olives.

When the pasta is al dente, drain it and add it to the pan with the fish. Sauté everything together briefly to finish cooking it. Add the basil and serve.

Wine suggestion: White – Lugana Riserva "Vigne di Catullo", Tenuta Roveglia (Turbiana)

Luccio alla Gardesana
Lake Garda Pike

This dish of flaked fish is served with polenta at Osteria dell'Orologio.

SERVES 6

Pike:
1 pike of around 2kg
1 carrot, halved
1 onion, halved
1 stick of celery, halved
1 clove garlic, peeled
5 bay leaves

Sauce:
1 glass of extra virgin olive oil
2 cloves garlic, finely chopped
6 anchovy fillets, finely chopped
50g capers, chopped
1 glass of vinegar
Handful of parsley, chopped

Poach the pike in salted water with the carrot, onion, celery, garlic and bay leaves for about 20 minutes.

In a separate pan, heat the oil then add the garlic, anchovies, capers and vinegar and stir until everything amalgamates and becomes a sauce.

Drain the fish, remove the skin and bones, and flake into separate piles per serving. Put a spoon of the sauce on top of the fish, sprinkle with parsley and serve.

Wine suggestion: Rosé – Valtenesi Chiaretto (Groppello, Sangiovese, Barbera)

Regional Specialities

Given the variety of its agricultural output, it's hardly surprising that Lombardy boasts a wealth of gastronomic specialities. From the rice plains and corn fields feeding the regional love of risotto and polenta, via the lakes providing fish and the microclimates where lemons and olives are cultivated, up to the mountains where cured meats such as bresaola and *violino di capra* are still made in the traditional way, it's a rich and diverse offering.

There are the excellent fruit and vegetables — Valtellina's apples, Mantua's melons and pears, Mezzago asparagus and Breme onions — and a wide variety of wines, from Lugana to Lambrusco Mantovano

with increasing international attention being paid to Franciacorta and the steep terraces of Valtellina where vineyards are defiantly nurtured on the steep south-facing slopes.

Cheese is made on the opposite side of the same valley, and Lombardy has 13 DOP cheeses — at the last count — including Grana Padano, Strachitunt, Quartirolo Lombardo and Taleggio, as well as many others of note such as Pannerone and Agrì di Valtorta.

We mustn't forget the international brands such as Campari, but alongside these are lots of small businesses that are equally, if quietly, proud of what they do and their contribution to Lombardy's gastronomic culture.

Bitto Storico
Paolo Ciapparelli

Centro del Bitto Storico
via Nazionale, 31
23010 Gerola Alta
T: +39 0342 690 081
W: formaggiobitto.com

The story of Bitto Storico is one of a traditionally made cheese that was struggling to survive against the onslaught of modernisation. Enter Paolo Ciapparelli, who, it's fair to say, is Bitto Storico's saviour. He was incensed that the age-old way of making Bitto was under threat and the number of traditional makers was dwindling. It's admittedly a challenging few months up on the pastures, and distinguishing your product from Bitto made by non-traditional methods (but which is DOP awarded) made life difficult.

He set about turning his exasperation into action, taking a practical rather than romantic approach. The first step was to pay the cheesemakers properly. Paolo's commitment to the cause was persuasive. Investors came on board despite his honest admission that "you won't get your money back if this doesn't succeed." And by 'succeed' he meant 'sell'.

Fittingly, it was a retired dairymaid who helped. She told Paolo that there was an unused building in Gerola Alta (a small village in the Valle del Bitto). After much work, he opened it in 2007 as the Centro del Bitto.

Today's makers use the same methods that their fathers and grandfathers did; hence the award of a Slow Food presidium. They and their herdsmen live up in the pastures with their cows and goats throughout the summer. All are from cheesemaking families and still use the milking stools and cheese forms of their forebears. Many of them are young, like Michele Lombella — albeit he has nearly 20 years' experience. He and his herdsmen work quickly and efficiently with little conversation. Twice a day they milk their grass-fed animals and make their wheels of cheese with 90% cow's and 10% goat's milk, using large pots suspended over open fires.

After a year, the cheeses are tapped so that their ability to age can be assessed. Up to ten years is the norm, but in Lombardy it's easy to meet people who have enjoyed much older Bitto Storico.

Paolo's Bitto Centre not only sells wheels of Bitto Storico but stores them for buyers while they age. "We don't just leave the cheese," explains Paolo. "It can't mature properly if not monitored. We need to deal with any damp periods." They also need to keep the rind clean so that the cheese can breathe. Each maker has a shelf in the Centre with their names and photo. Many purchasers come back periodically to see how their wheel is maturing — and often to pose for an annual family photo with the changing wheel (it loses 35% of its weight in the first three years).

The cheesemakers know not just Paolo but the other people who work in the Bitto Centre — people such as Albino Mazzolini, and Gloria Maxenti, whose father was a cheesemaker. It's a very close-knit community on the shady side of the Valtellina. Of course on the opposite side of the valley, the side that sees the sunshine, the focus is on wine. What could be better than a vertical tasting of Chiavennasca and Bitto Storico together?

Opposite top left: Michele Lombella

Above centre: The cheese forms

Bresaola
Aldo and Enrico Del Curto

Macelleria Del Curto
via Dolzino, 129
23022 Chiavenna
T: +39 0343 32312

Chiavenna is a delightful town — obviously, it's in the Valchiavenna.
However, it offers the added pleasure of palm trees with a view of snow-
covered Alps in the distance.

It's also the home of Macelleria Del Curto, a butcher's shop set up in 1902.
Currently run by Aldo with his brother Enrico and the latter's son Daniele,
the shop is known not just for top quality butchery but for its bresaola and
violino di capra. Before becoming retailers, the family farmed livestock and
then moved into butchering. Establishing a shop was the logical next step.

The salted, air-dried and aged beef called bresaola (or *brisaola* in the local
dialect) is a speciality of both the Valchiavenna and the Valtellina. At Del
Curto, they cure their beef for bresaola in premises behind the retail shop,
ensuring that the strong smell of ammonia generated by the curing process
is kept away from the customers. Daniele explains that "most of the beef we
use here comes from Germany and France," but does not reveal the exact
mix of salt, and seasonings; here, as with other bresaola producers it's a
closely guarded secret.

They are also highly regarded for their *violino di capra*, a local speciality with
a Slow Food presidium. Produced from goat leg and shoulder, it has to cure
for at least 60 days. It is shaped like a violin, and held like one when it's
carved — hence the name.

Bresaola
Stefano Masanti and Matteo Maglio

MA! Officina Gastronomica
via A. De Giacomi 7
23024 Madesimo
T: +39 0343 53025
W: maofficinagastronomica.com

Stefano Masanti is the chef at the Michelin-starred Il Cantinone in the ski resort town of Madesimo in the Valchiavenna. He started making bresaola — and excellent *violino di capra* — for the restaurant and, encouraged by diners, made more for sale.

With Matteo Maglio, he's transformed the site of a former supermarket into state-of-the-art premises for drying and curing. But there are no modern tricks: no chemicals are used, only salt. The beef for bresaola spends one week at a temperature of 24-25°C with low (30%) humidity. The conditions are controlled by a sensor. After the first week the temperature goes down and the humidity up each day until 14°C and 80% is reached. They age their bresaola longer than many other producers: a minimum of 45 days and a maximum of 150. Many producers lose only 30% of the weight of their meat; they lose 50-60%.

The sheer quantity of bresaola produced in northern Lombardy means, Stefano explains, that "most of the beef comes from South American breeds." But he and Matteo are keen to keep it local. They're working with some academics to improve traceability. "Our bresaola will come with a QR code showing details on where and how the animal was raised and cured," he says.

If you're in Madesimo when Il Cantinone is open, try Stefano's white *pizzoccheri* "because we don't have buckwheat here." But don't fail to enjoy the bresaola and *violino di capra*.

Rice
Pietro Schiavi

**Riseria F.lli Schiavi Snc
via Boccalina, 5
46040 Castiglione Mantovano di Roverbella
T: +39 0376 697 023**

Rice is important in both Lombard cooking — think classics such as *risotto alla Milanese* — and agriculture: paddy fields stretch verdantly along the southern belt of the region through Mantua and Pavia. Although there are lots of large processing companies, some small rice mills still exist; Pietro Schiavi runs one that was founded in 1687.

His grandfather bought the mill, which was passed to his father, Giuseppe, and uncles. But his father died as Pietro was about to head off to university and his mother insisted that he continue the family business. So he stayed put, learning everything about rice milling from his uncle Fiorindo. Pietro may feel a little regret about this, but no bitterness. "Working here makes me happy and as the years go by, I like it even more," he says.

Today he mills the rice of nearby growers. Nothing is wasted. The removed husks are, he says, "put on the ground to make chickens comfortable," and the chaff is used for fodder. Damaged grains are removed and used for animal feed or milled again for rice flour. Only half of the delivered weight of paddy ends up as finished rice by the end of the milling and sorting processes.

"Friends with modern rice mills come here and are nostalgic for how things used to be," says Pietro. That's understandable because the current mill was made before 1900. There are still a few artisans who can repair it when it has problems, however. The ancient separator works because the grains with husks travel at a different speed from those without, so they get sent in different directions. "It's a simple machine with no electronic programming," says Pietro. "Why do you need to complicate things? Simple is always best."

Unsurprisingly he is a big rice fan, believing that it is "one of nature's health givers — the best thing to eat if you're not feeling well." He also values every grain. "If you want to eat leftover cooked rice, use a non-stick pan and reheat it," he insists. This may not be universally seen as good food hygiene but he responds, "These rumours are invented by people who have too much money and don't care about wasting good food."

Top left: Pietro makes running repairs to his machinery

Top right: Pietro Schiavi

Grana Padano

Consorzio Tutela Grana Padano
via XXIV Giugno, 8
25015 San Martino della Battaglia
Desenzano del Garda
W: granapadano.it

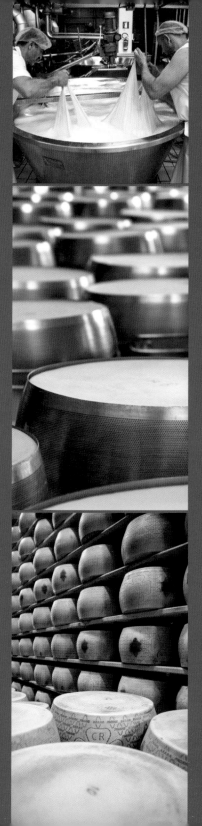

"Grana Padano is fundamentally important to the cuisine and heritage of this region," explains Nicola Cesare Baldrighi. He happens to be President of the Grana Padano Consorzio, but nonetheless, it's hard to disagree. Throughout Lombardy it's included in recipes, grated over food and served in rough edged nuggets for an umami hit with *aperitivi*.

Grana Padano was created by Benedictine monks who, to avoid wasting surplus milk, needed to find a way to use it; today's producers of the cheese are proud of the fact that the original recipe "has not really changed," as one puts it. Given the belief that the first Grana Padano cheese was produced in 1135, that's quite something, although he adds, "It's been adapted according to technological advances. Temperatures are no longer checked with elbows."

Its name comes from the cheese's grainy quality — '*formaggio di grana*' is used as a general term — and 'Padano' specifies that it's made in the Po Valley, 'La Pianura Padana'. For a long time it was a seasonal cheese, only produced in spring and summer when there was enough spare milk. That's no longer the case. It's now not only the world's bestselling DOP (in English, Protected Designation of Origin) cheese, but the bestselling DOP product, with annual production approaching five million wheels and involving over 50,000 workers. High profile among these is the maestro responsible for the *battitura*, the tapping of the wheel.

But it's Grana's versatility that helps to explain how widespread it is throughout the region and why so many chefs and home cooks find it indispensable. Comparisons with Parmigiano Reggiano, or Parmesan, are inevitable, especially as part of the DOP area for Parmesan extends into the south-eastern part of Lombardy around Mantua. One reason why many opt for Grana Padano though, is because it can be aged for less time. There are

three maturity bands of Grana Padano, the oldest being over 20 months. But using the youngest, aged between 9 -16 months, means that it doesn't overpower other flavours. Old or young, however, it is aptly described — by a worker in the PLAC (Produttori Latte Associati Cremona) plant — as having "taste with personality."

Goose
Gioachino Palestro

Corte dell'Oca
via Sforza, 27
27036 Mortara
T: +39 0384 98397
www.cortedelloca.com

The Lomellina area includes the towns of Vigevano (with its spectacular piazza) and charming Mortara. But it is perhaps better known for goose.

Geese were reared in this area centuries ago to meet demand from the local Jewish population. Demand, as Gioachino Palestro will tell you, has grown a lot since then. He has been an enthusiastic champion for everything to do with geese for decades. He started as a butcher and now runs the Corte dell'Oca in the centre of Mortara where goose meat is prepared, preserved and promoted. And he is the most dedicated of promoters. Around town, he animatedly introduces people who use his goose fat: a baker who makes goose-shaped bread (although not in the summer), and a *pasticceria* where they use it for the shortest, crumbliest biscuits, also appropriately shaped.

However, Gioachino is an ardent fan of one breed in particular: the *bianca romagnola*. It is, he says, very intelligent and has "the finest meat with the best balance of fat. Nothing else compares."

In mid June he prepares to move his 12-day-old goslings to their home in the open air where they'll remain until they're ready for eating in winter and "perfect for Christmas." They're fed corn, grass and rice damaged in the harvest, then fattened up with dried figs brought in especially from Puglia, Calabria and Sicily. But first there's All Saints Day, and goose is a traditional food on the first of November. You don't have to eat it fresh though; there's a wide range of salumi and ways of preserving goose such as *salame d'oca di Mortara*, IGP and *petto e prosciuttino d'oca*.

Polenta
Sergio and Marco Bruciamonti

Molino Bruciamonti Siro Snc
via Roma, 50
27047 Santa Maria della Versa
T: +39 0385 278 010

Polenta has long been a staple food in Lombardy and elsewhere in northern Italy. Although the word can refer to any mix of ground cereal with water, these days it usually means corn.

At Molino Bruciamonti, Sergio and Marco's grandparents started milling corn to make various types of polenta grain and flour back in 1936. The brothers now run the mill together and are proud of the fact that their ancient machinery still gives such good results.

Harvested in September, the kernels are cut from the corn cobs and dried quickly at a low temperature to prevent a smoked taste. The corn is then milled between two stones, only one of which moves. To make fine flour, *farina di grano turco*, the process is repeated using stones that are closer together.

Polenta is traditionally cooked in a copper pan with a rounded bottom, and in the past was often stirred with long homemade wooden implements. These days most professional kitchens have an electric *paiolo* with a revolving paddle, which saves the physically demanding and time-consuming work of vigorous stirring.

Sergio clearly loves polenta. He also has some useful advice. "If you go somewhere and want to eat well, then eat like the locals. Don't go to Switzerland and complain that you don't think much of their spaghetti with clams." That's a good enough reason to choose polenta in the Oltrepò Pavese.

Campari

Galleria Campari
viale Gramsci, 161
20099 Sesto San Giovanni
T: +39 02 62251
W: campari.com

Campari: Milan's *aperitivo* of choice since 1860. Well, perhaps not quite that long but that's the year the firm was founded. And the year that Gaspare Campari invented the bitter-tasting, vivid red aperitif. He'd arrived in Milan to work as a waiter but had far more success opening a small shop selling alcohol. He started to invent and make spirits, elixirs, vermouths and, importantly, bitters. The rest is (alcoholic) history.

Campari, the drink, is still a very closely guarded secret infusion of herbs alcohol and water, and — perhaps — some mystery ingredients too. What is clear is that lots of mixologists find Campari indispensable, whether for a classic Negroni (Campari, gin and sweet vermouth) or for a personal creation. It's also frequently referred to as "an acquired taste"; however it's drunk, its bitterness does polarise opinion.

What's difficult to dispute is that since the beginning it's been a very visual brand. In fact, it's hard to imagine Campari without its association with strong, vibrant and arresting images. But then Milan is a design capital. The current logo may be internationally recognised but a variety of different lettering was tried out before choosing it. Looking back through the archive of posters is an education in visual art.

And as part of the contemporary approach, there was close working alongside the Futurists. The movement, which looked to the future, loathed anything representing the past and supported technological advancement. Visually, Futurists favoured geometric shapes and strong colours and saw advertising as a helpful way of reaching a wide audience. It was a perfect mix. Futurist artist Fortunato Depero worked on a number of advertisements for the brand and designed the Campari Soda bottle in 1932 which is still in production today.

Gaspare Campari died in 1882, and it was his fourth child, Davide, born in 1867 who creatively and astutely transformed the brand, being responsible for a lot of what we associate it with today. If further proof were needed that Campari is part of the interacting, socialising culture of Milan, Davide Campari was the first local citizen to be born in the Galleria Vittorio Emanuele. You don't get much more Milanese than that.

Franciacorta Wines
www.franciacorta.net

In the centre of Lombardy, to the south of Lake Iseo, is Franciacorta. In the 1950s, this vine-covered landscape produced predominantly red wines. It's one of the more extraordinary wine area evolutions that, in mere decades, it has become the home of Italy's best fizz. Franciacorta is made from varying combinations of Chardonnay, Pinot Blanc and Pinot Noir, but the word Franciacorta refers not just to the wine and the place but also the method of production — as does Champagne.

Controls for production are strict and those involved in Franciacorta winemaking are proud of the regulations that they adhere to; secondary

fermentation in the bottle is essential. What is up for choice is the type of Franciacorta: Brut, Non Dosato, Satèn (from the word for silk), Rosé (Pinot Noir has to be at least 25 per cent of the cuvée) and Millesimato (vintage). There's also a focus on sustainability, the environmental impact of wine production and reducing pesticide use.

Aside from wine there's good food from an ever-increasing number of artisan producers and restaurants — both smart and casual. And there's a healthy support of artistic innovation: Ca' del Bosco winery has an 'art garden' with dramatic modern sculptures and Bellavista is a supporter of cultural initiatives at La Scala. Bellavista's Francesca Moretti sums it up, "Making wine," she says, "is an artistic expression."

Bellavista Winery
Francesca Moretti

Bellavista
via Bellavista 5
Erbusco 25030
+39 030 776 2000
www.bellavistawine.it

"I grew up here, on this hill," reflects Francesca Moretti. "When I was a child, it was normal for me to be with someone in the winery or the vineyard." Like so many of the great Italian chefs — often influenced by their formative experiences of cooking at kitchen tables with their mothers — there was perhaps an inevitability about Francesca being drawn to a professional life in the family wineries.

But first Francesca went to university and studied not only oenology but viticulture. Even today, she may be found among the vines, catching moments of reflection in the open air.

As a woman who oversees one of the most highly regarded names in Franciacorta, as well as the other family wineries, she's refreshingly straightforward about the wine world and the strides forward that women are making. She's not one for gender clichés but is clear on why women have certain advantages over men in wine making. "We have a different sensibility and are more predisposed to adapt ourselves to whatever nature gives us, in the same way that a mother accepts a child — no matter what," she explains. "I see the same thing in wine: we accept a harvest, however it turns out."

But Francesca also has a flair for design and, influenced by the bubbles in Franciacorta and the association of fizz and merrymaking, decided to change the — slightly formal — labels on the Bellavista bottles to reflect the brightness and vibrancy of the natural world.

Multi-award-winning oenologist Mattia Vezzola, who has a long-standing working relationship with Bellavista, is serious about the technicalities of wine making, but he too is keen to embrace the celebratory aspect of

Franciacorta explaining, with his trademark twinkly smile, that "celebrating a wedding anniversary should involve drinking a bottle of Bellavista — one for each year."

Francesca's upbringing, acquired knowledge and expertise have given her the perfect combination of skills and sensibilities in a world that combines agriculture, science and creativity. But for her it always comes back to nature. And her nearest and dearest. "My values were passed on to me by my parents," she says. "I was brought up to appreciate and respect the environment. Bellavista is a reflection of my family."

Above left: Mattia Vezzola

Above right: Francesca Moretti

Berlucchi Winery
Franco Ziliani

Guido Berlucchi & C.
Piazza Duranti, 4
25040 Borgonato
T: +39 030 984 381
W: berlucchi.it

Franco Ziliani wanted a job he enjoyed, and found it — through a chance remark to a colleague. Coming from a family of wine sellers, he studied oenology and soon after he qualified, his newly acquired expertise was needed by Guido Berlucchi, a nearby winery owner. The two discussed various wine issues and Franco, who was a student of Champagne, ventured the idea that they could make top quality fizz where they were. And so began the sparkling wine story of Franciacorta.

Now in his mid 80s, Franco's been around for long enough to have his own ideas and to acknowledge that he swims against the tide sometimes. He's not, for example, a big fan of endless fanciful taste descriptions. "I'm convinced that if you're honest about the first thing you taste in a wine, it's grapes," he says. "Before exotic fruits and apples, it's grapes!" He also prefers his Franciacorta served at 5-6°C. "The gourmets say 8°C but I prefer it a bit colder, especially on a hot day." But he is with the consensus that Franciacorta matches well with most foods ("apart from grapes – and chocolate").

Since those days of suggesting fizz to Guido Berlucchi, he's seen big changes in the area — and he knows that, as he puts it, "the people here deserve their success. The rapid evolution over 25-30 years is down to the hard work and sacrifices of the people in Franciacorta."

He may no longer be a youngster, but Franco Ziliani still bubbles with enthusiasm — and playfulness. He's amusing and charismatic, modestly refers to himself as lucky, and laughs easily. He continues to enjoy research trips to the top houses of Champagne, these days with friends, and is a big fan of "music — and dancing." Knowing that his winery is in the capable

and hard-working hands of his children, Arturo, Paolo and Cristina, it would be easy for him to slow down but, he says, "I still think of things I want to do because I so love my work. I'll never stop."

He has indeed enjoyed his professional life — a combination of extraordinary achievements and lots of good times. "Fun is very good for your health" he smiles. "And I'm still having fun."

Ca' del Bosco Winery
Maurizio Zanella

Ca' del Bosco
via Albano Zanella, 13
25030 Erbusco
T: +39 030 776 6111
W: cadelbosco.com

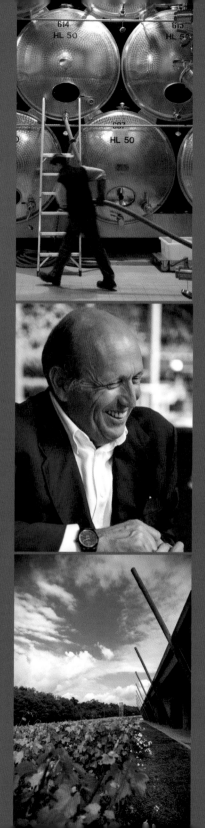

The original Ca' del Bosco — the House in the Woods — was a small dwelling with uncertain access and no electricity or running water. It's still on the site of the Franciacorta winery to which it gives its name but, since Maurizio Zanella's mother bought it, has become a great deal more habitable.

Just as well for Maurizio who, in his teenage years, was 'exiled' there (his father was exasperated with his son's youthful high jinks). From the centre of Milan to a rural house with chickens and fruit trees was something of a leap, but it was the few vines and the small amount of family wine making that led to Maurizio being invited on a trip to study the vineyards of France. He wasn't interested in the winemaking at all, but the lure of two days in Paris had him packing his bag.

The first stop for the bus transporting our young rebel and a bunch of ageing Lombard vineyard owners was at Domaine de la Romanée-Conti. Maurizio had to be persuaded to enter, but he saw the cellar, tasted the wine and "I bought three bottles."

That was the end of his money for the week, but the start of a new direction. Back home, he now had a real purpose: making quality wine. His father helped him get organised but let him plough his own furrow. Maurizio went on, over the decades, to build up an extraordinary winery. Alongside the celebrated wines there's a striking quantity of art, especially sculpture because, he explains, "I love the way it's three-dimensional in the same way that wine has colour, smell and taste." And he's also a photography devotee. Coincidentally, when Helmut Newton turned up with his models to shoot among the vines, so did lots of field workers.

These days the winery has an impressive range of modern technology. "It helps us to be more traditional," says Maurizio. "We want to do things the way they were done a long time ago, but in an easier way." But he understands the importance of people, "Wine making is manual work so lots of hands are needed to make great wine. A good team is essential." And a visionary leader.

Opposite centre: Maurizio Zanella

Ferghettina Winery
Laura and Matteo Gatti

Azienda Agricola
Ferghettina di Roberto
Gatti
via Saline, 11
25030 Adro
T: +39 030 745 1212
W: ferghettina.it

"Selling wine is not just about the product, but the emotion associated with it," says Laura Gatti, daughter of Roberto, who founded her family's winery, Ferghettina. Her father had worked in wine for decades so Laura and her brother Matteo were brought up "counting the years by grape harvests," as she puts it.

Laura knew from watching her father how demanding and tiring the work was; after graduating from Milan as an oenologist, she understood how technically difficult and complicated it is too.

But she loves the stimulation — the challenge of combining her own creativity and the unpredictability of nature. Nevertheless, being able to work outside, and "follow nature's rhythms," is one of the best parts of her job. She loves the buzz of harvest time when everyone pulls together to get the work done and she becomes almost sentimental when talking about the joys of "following the vines from their flowering, seeing the growth of the grapes, picking them and ultimately ending up with a year's work in a glass."

But Laura isn't the only oenologist of her generation in the family. Her brother Matteo, who works alongside her, came up with the idea of the winery's square-based bottles, used to give more surface contact for the Rosé and Milledì wines.

Their father is still committed to, and enthusiastic about, his work and winery. "He gets up at 5 in the morning and continues until 8 in the evening, frequently without stopping," says Laura. But when Roberto does pause, Pietro, Laura's young son, is a fun distraction.

Roberto has bought his grandson pairs of sheep, donkeys, peacocks, geese, ducks and chickens, so he can learn about looking after animals. And there's every sign that Pietro will continue in his grandfather's footsteps. Certainly he loves "playing at winemaking."

Which is promising because the intention is to keep Ferghettina as a family winery. "We don't want to increase the quantity of wine,' says Laura. "We want to stay a family firm. We're used to looking after every detail ourselves. We may be small but people respect us. It wouldn't be the same if we became too big."

Valtellina Wines

www.stradavinivaltellina.com

The Valtellina is the Adda River valley, running from east to west. The shady side is known for its cheese. Along the sunny side are the sub-zones of the Valtellina Superiore appellation (DOCG): Sassella, Inferno, Grumello, Valgella and Maroggia. Sforzato, or Sfursat di Valtellina, also has a DOCG but requires naturally dried grapes, 90% of which must be Chiavennasca (the local name for Nebbiolo).

Recent years have seen many young, qualified winemakers eager to take on the challenging conditions — but they need to be energetic. With steep slopes, some said to range from 45% up to 65%, everything is

done manually and requires several times the usual number of winemaking hours per hectare.

But it's a close-knit group whose members have a strong and proud attachment to their homeland. For all the demands, many locals feel 'embraced by the mountains' and hope that small producers will thrive because it gives a distinctive feel to their *territorio*.

As you drive through the valley, winery names appear, Hollywood style, in large letters on the hillsides. Except that here you're more likely to find hard-working, authentic and grounded characters than Tinseltown wannabes. As winemaker Marco Fay says, "We're mountain people here." Maybe they are, but their wines frequently steal the limelight.

ARPEPE Winery
Emanuele and Isabella Pelizzatti Perego

ARPEPE
via Del Buon Consiglio, 4
23100 Sondrio
T: +39 0342 214 120
W: arpepe.com

As a young boy, Emanuele Pelizzatti Perego was certain that he didn't want to work in his family's winery. He hated the smell of the cellar so much that he trained to be a *geometra*. But after three years of surveying and building he realised it wasn't for him. And despite himself, he was becoming increasingly interested in the changes his father was making to the winery.

Meanwhile, his sister Isabella had studied science and technology, then completed a masters in oenology before working for an international drinks corporation where she was responsible for "creating products that met the needs of the market." She's happy that now the requirement is reversed, namely that, "we have a great product, we just need to bring it to market." But she adds, "I always knew that the mountain Nebbiolo wine that we make in the Valtellina was very special." She returned home in 2001 to work with Emanuele. Today the two of them, with their brother Guido, run the ARPEPE winery, the fifth generation of the family to do so.

That continuation isn't as straightforward as it sounds: in 1973 their father sold the company, cellar, wine and brand. But not the vineyards. Deciding to start again a few years later, he repurchased part of the cellar and returned to his vines. Fans of his wine had to be patient though. It was six years before he was willing to present a bottle for sale.

Traditional wine ageing is still important but in contrast the winery is sleekly modern; Emanuele wanted something bright next to the original part, which is embedded in the hillside — contemporary architecture that, he believes, shows people how open to innovation they are. He also has a

Above: Emanuele and Isabella

particular attachment to their Rosso di Valtellina. "In my opinion it's the wine that changed our winery," he explains. "The first one was made in 2003 — and that was the first harvest that I oversaw."

Isabella points out that their wines "seem easy to drink but they have a complexity which makes them intriguing." She's also fascinated by the ageing potential of wine and cheese. "I love the microbiology behind both," she says.

The siblings spend a lot of time together these days, especially when it comes to tasting and deciding how long to age their highly respected wines. Emanuele recognises that "every passionate producer is an ambassador of the *territorio*." It's a good job that his dislike of the cellar is long gone, and he's aware — constantly — that "we truly have some amazing vines in our hands."

Above: Emanuele and Isabella

Dirupi Winery
Pierpaolo Di Franco and Davide Fasolini

Dirupi SA
via San Carlo
Località Madonna di
Campagna
23026 Ponte in Valtellina
T: +39 347 290 9779
W: dirupi.com

Back in 2003 you'd have had to be very pro-risk to put money on Davide Fasolini and Pierpaolo Di Franco's start-up winery. Even their university friends joked that they wouldn't last a year together. "You can't even agree on posts for the vines," they said. Oh, and they had no vines.

What they did have was an extraordinary amount of energy and "a dream," says Davide — "a dream about our very own bottles." So, they persuaded vineyard owners to let them look after their vines, worked all the hours they could through the week, and made ends meet in a pizzeria and a bar at the weekend.

They met studying winemaking at university. Pierpaolo had previously studied *geometra* with Emanuele of ARPEPE, and Davide's route was even less predictable. "I like to party," he explains, "and I'd help a friend's uncle with his harvest because there was always a big party afterwards. I associated discussions on viticulture with having a really good time, but then I understood that it was more than that." Out of the classroom he also learnt quickly that "nature teaches you that you have to do things at the right time, otherwise everything becomes much more difficult."

In fact at the beginning, says Pierpaolo, "the older generations who entrusted their vines to us got cross because they thought we weren't doing things properly." "Remember," adds Davide "that we began work in 2004 when I was 23 and Pierpaolo was 25 so we had 48 years between us and we were working with plants that were almost 100 years old."

But they've proved themselves and "now people who are so much older than us want to know all about our methods. We've been learning from each other," he smiles proudly.

And after all the hard work, there's a post-harvest party tradition to maintain, explains Davide. "It's our way of thanking everyone who has helped us throughout the year."

They're still very different. "I like provoking and I'm a bit scatter-brained," Davide says. "Pierpaolo's solid, dependable and very precise." But they do have two things in common. One is luscious locks. "We both keep our hair long because our dads are bald, so it's only a matter of time," shrugs Pierpaolo.

And they always agreed on the sorts of wines they liked — and wanted to make. "We want people to taste the grapes and know that the wine we make can only come from Valtellina."

Above left: Davide Fasolini

Above right: Pierpaolo Di Franco

Fay Winery
Marco Fay

Società Agricola Fay
via Pila Caselli, 1
23036 San Giacomo di
Teglio
T: +39 0342 786 071
W: vinifay.it

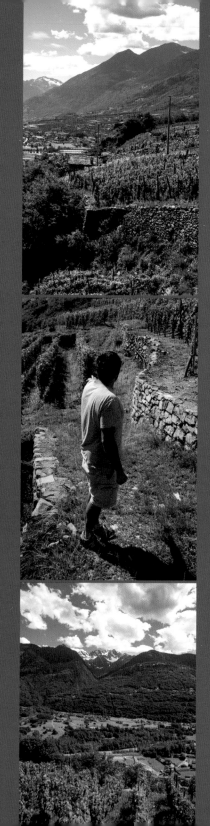

Sandro Fay decided in 1971 that he'd build his own winery. He'd been working in the Veneto for the best part of a decade, but then returned to Valtellina. Two years later, the Fay winery opened.

Sandro's father had run a grocery store and produced wine for sale there. It was the wine rather than the food that interested his son. In turn, Marco, Sandro's son, knew from the age of ten that he wanted to make wine. "If you grow up in a winery, you can't help but understand that the harvest is an important moment for the family," he explains.

Marco chose to train at the San Michele all'Adige institute, after which he studied oenology at university in Milan. For all the knowledge he gained there, his boundless and ardent enthusiasm for his *territorio* was cultivated at home. So despite his workload he needs little encouragement to jump in his car and hurtle like a rally driver along the hairpin bends of the slopes around Chiuro and Teglio, in order to explain — and show — the different sub-zones of Chiavennasca cultivation.

"We start with great grapes," he says. "I look at them at harvest time and I know what will result." This made it hard in 2008 when the grapes promised little. "I didn't know what to do, so I didn't produce anything." It was an onerous decision from an economic point of view, but he wasn't prepared to compromise. "I was lucky because that's the one difficult year I've had," he says. "My father had more."

He's also keen to convey the other challenges nature offers, "There's a rhythm to working with vines that depends on the weather," he says. "There are times when it rains that these slopes won't permit us to go out." Standing on a particularly steep bank, he adds, "I always say that here in the Valtellina we have a *territorio* that is much stronger than man."

He knows this is a challenging business. But he also knows that increasing numbers of wine connoisseurs from far away appreciate his wine. "People like our house style, which is clean and elegant," and he adds, "Nebbiolo is seen as being very Italian."

Above right: Marco Fay

Nino Negri Winery
Casimiro Maule

Casa Vinicola Nino Negri
via Ghibellini, 3
23030 Chiuro
T: +39 0342 485 211
W: ninonegri.it

"As everybody knows," says Casimiro Maule, "wine is made on the vine, not in the winery." Nowadays regarded as the revered elder statesman of the Valtellina, Casimiro started work at Nino Negri (where wine has been made since 1897) when Carlo Negri hired him from the agrarian school of San Michele all'Adige in 1972 — so he knows better than most how things have changed. He remembers, for instance, the days when casks were used continually for 50 or even 100 years, and so developed mould. "You'd taste a wine, remark that it had some faults and be told, 'No, it's typical.' You'd — rightly — never get away with that these days."

He's happy that youngsters are now returning to the countryside and winemaking, "not for great financial gain but for great satisfaction." He sees the exchange of ideas as important and is ready to share his experience. "We have an extraordinary viticulture here with ten centuries of history," he says, adding, "It's an antique viticulture and we're modernising it." That said, he considers sustainability to be critical but he's not at all wide-eyed about it. Whatever your thoughts on environmental best practice, he suggests, economic sustainability is the key. "I'm a frugal man and a winery that loses money will close," he says. "You need continual investment to keep improving because quality is made with money."

He's only too aware that one of the major costs here is the walls that prevent landslides on the slopes. The safety and comfort of staff is critically important to him of course but in any case, the investment is also worthwhile because, he points out, "If you need to rebuild a collapsed wall, then it will take you 100 years to recuperate that cost."

Those steep slopes are challenging but ultimately rewarding for the dedicated winemaker. Casimiro's always travelled a lot and "I try as many foreign wines as I can to see what they're like and how they've been made,"

he explains. "I keep myself up to date because there's always a need to understand what is happening elsewhere."

Even if he is unable to say which of the wines he's produced is his favourite, he's particularly proud of his white, Ca' Brione, made from Chiavannesca, Sauvignon, Chardonnay and Incrocio Manzoni grapes. But perhaps the one that gave him the most pleasure was the Sforzato Cinque Stelle "because," he says, "it's the wine that made me understand that it's possible to make great wines in the Valtellina."

Opposite top: Casimiro Maule

Bernina Express "Trenino Rosso"

W: rhb.ch/en/panoramic-
trains/bernina-express

Many people think the Bernina Express route is the most beautiful train ride in the world. Whether it is or not, taking the *trenino rosso*, the 'little red train' as it's affectionately called, from Tirano at the eastern end of the valley and travelling through dramatically changing scenery over a couple of hours to arrive at St Moritz invariably prompts words like 'breathtaking'. And it certainly brings home the fact that the Italian Valtellina lies right next to Switzerland.

The on-board ticket inspectors are a friendly bunch. They pass on nuggets of advice such as, "autumn is the best time to travel on this route as it's still hot and sunny in Tirano but there's already snow up high, so you see all the seasons in one ride."

During the summer months, there's the option of sitting in an open yellow carriage attached to the back of the train. But be warned — however warm it is in Tirano, the temperature drops considerably as you reach the mountains. There's the choice of a carriage with big glass windows, although you should be aware that these don't open if your intention is to take photos. Should you wish to do this, buy a ticket for one of the standard carriages.

The quaint town of Tirano comes to a halt for train arrivals and departures. At least part of the street does. That's because the railway line goes down it. Not alongside it, but down the very centre of the street, past the chocolate box Santuario della Madonna di Tirano church. All but the most distracted or jaded locals are used to waving back at excited visitors setting off on their train ride.

After gliding through the town centre, the train then passes through cow-dotted fields, alongside waterfalls and on to mountains, lakes and pine forests as it twists and turns, sometimes dramatically. Occasional announcements and recordings are played over the PA system regarding noteworthy facts such as the height of the next landmark. As time goes by

the language changes from Italian to German. Advance warning is given before reaching the circular viaduct at Brusio which enables the train to climb.

And climb it does — all the way up to Ospizio Bernina at 2253 metres. From up there you can see valley floors with their human imprints: a few roads, some barns, hamlets, maybe even a building whose purpose is impossible to work out before you've passed it.

Which is why red lights are welcome as they give you a chance to take in the scenery — and know that another red train will imminently pass. Parts of the landscape start to feel bleak, even lunar at times, and although everything seems big, there's often no reference point for scale. Then the train descends and the Swiss flags gradually disappear on the approach back to Tirano in Lombardy. It's an awe-inspiring and delightful round-trip.

The most beautiful train ride in the world? It surely has to be a contender.

Glossary

Many specialities and terms are explained in the body of the text but here are details — or additional details — on some which may require further explanation. All refer to the content of this book.

Agrì di Valtorta: a small cheese made with raw cow's milk produced throughout the year in Valtorta in the province of Bergamo. It has a Slow Food Presidium

Allevamento: a breeding farm or ranch; livestock

Asiago: a cow's milk cheese from the town of the same name in the Veneto

Asparago di Cilavegna: asparagus from the province of Pavia which has purple tips. It is prized for its flavour

Bagòss di Bagolino: a strong flavoured cheese from the province of Brescia. It is often grilled and eaten with polenta

Barricato: describes wines that have been aged in barriques

Biancostato: a cut of beef from the stomach which is used in *bollito misto*

Bitto DOP: cheese made from cow's and goat's milk

Bitto Storico: this cheese is produced only during the summer. It is aged for a minimum of 12 months and frequently up to ten years. It has a Slow Food Presidium

Bollicine: literally "bubbles", so 'bubbly' or 'fizz' in reference to sparkling wines

Bollito misto: a traditional Lombard dish of various meats which are simmered in a stock until tender. Some restaurants still serve it from a special trolley which is wheeled to the table

Bottarga: salted and dried fish roe

Bottega: a small shop

Branzi: a mountain cheese produced in the summer

Buckwheat: produced in the Valtellina where the best is said to come from the area around Teglio. It is used for *pizzoccheri* pasta and added to cornmeal polenta, along with butter and cheese for *polenta taragna*

Cappone: capon

Cascina: farm or farmstead

Casera DOP: a cheese from Valtellina, 'Casera' refers to the house or cellar in which the cheese was aged. In the past, Valtellina Casera was only made in the winter; summer milk was used for Bitto

Cassoeula, cazzoeûla (or several other spellings): a traditional Lombard winter stew using pig's ears, tail, feet and pork rind

Chiavennasca: the Valtellina name for Nebbiolo

Ciccioli d'oca: goose scratchings or cracklings

Coda: tail

Fatulì della Val Saviore: a small production goat's cheese from the Val Camonica in Brescia. It has a Slow Food Presidium

Gorgonzola DOP: a blue veined cheese made from cow's milk and popular in many countries. It takes its name from the town near Milan

Grano saraceno: buckwheat

Granoturco: maize

Imbarcadero: landing stage where the lake ferries stop

Lardo: cured pig's fat

Lavarello: a lake fish

Lungolago: the lake front or route around the lake

Macelleria: butcher's shop

Malfatti: these dumplings of spinach, cheese, flour, breadcrumbs and egg yolks, are cooked in boiling water and usually served with melted butter and sage. Malfatti literally means 'badly made'

Miccone: bread from the Oltrepò Pavese

Orto: a vegetable garden

Paiolo: traditionally a deep copper pan with a round bottom used for making polenta. Today, most professional kitchens have an electric *paiolo* which is a motorised stirring paddle on a copper pot

Pancetta rotolata: rolled pancetta served as an antipasto

Pannerone: sometimes referred to as 'white Gorgonzola', it's produced throughout the year. Pannerone di Lodi has a Slow Food presidium

Panettone di Milano: a large, light cake with dried fruit and candied peel which is eaten at Christmas and enjoyed increasingly outside of Italy

Quartirolo Lombardo: a cow's milk cheese. The term refers to the grass that grew after the third harvest of hay — the last before winter set in — and was called the 'quartirolo' or 'fourth cut'

Robiola: a soft cow's milk cheese

Salumi: plural of salume and the general term for cured meats

Slow Food Presidium: protection and support programmes by the Slow Food Foundation for foods considered to be of historical importance that are made by artisan producers using traditional methods

Sorbir d'agnoli: filled pasta parcels served in hot, wine enhanced stock

Spalla cotta: cured pork shoulder that has been cooked

Spiedo Bresciano or Spiedo alla bresciana: traditionally in Brescia especially in the Val Camonica, Val Trompia and Valle Sabbia, a skewer of small birds cooked over the fireplace. These days the skewer features less controversial meats such as pork, chicken and rabbit

Stoccafisso: stockfish or fish preserved by air drying and without the use of salt

Strachitunt: a cheese of ancient origins made in the Val Taleggio

Stracchino all'antica delle valli orobiche: a cow's milk cheese of ancient origins which is now made throughout the year and is considered to be a predecessor of Strachitunt and Taleggio. It has a Slow Food Presidium

Taleggio DOP: soft, creamy cheese from the Val Taleggio

Tortelli di Zucca: pasta parcels that are filled with squash and crushed almond biscuits then served with butter

Violino di capra: cured leg of goat which is carved by holding like a violin —hence the name

Index

Acknowledgements

The author would like to thank: Everybody who has helped to bring this book to completion, especially everyone in Lombardy, all the chefs, owners, front of house staff, producers and winemakers who welcomed, informed and assisted us in ways which are too many to count; individuals at the Regione di Lombardia who took time to meet with me when I was finding my feet, Giuseppe De Vita, Folco Ciulli, Rosangela Morana, Francesca Ossola, Silvana Ceresoli and their colleagues; Paolo Marchi and Elisa Zanotti of Identità Golose for generous help and introductions; all at Bonny Day especially Elizabeth Canning, Isabel Whitley and Scott Berry; enormous thanks to Vaughan O'Grady for being an encouraging and constructive editor, always with a calm head and dry witticism; Andrea Bothamley for meticulous proof reading; Caroline Shaw and Jane Livesey for sanity restoring evenings out; Giacomo Mojoli who has an incomparable understanding of Italy's current gastronomy and generously gave me invaluable guidance; Richard and Natalie Bone, Susan Searle and Pete Livesey who recipe tested with tenacity, alongside Jane Baxter — one of my favourite people to eat and drink with in Italy, while back home, she and the other #SODs (you know who you are) are still the best Negroni drinking group in town; Celia Plender for diligent recipe editing; Strada del Franciacorta especially Gabriella Campese and her colleagues for their assistance; Bryony Wright for help with Franciacorta in the UK; Michele Forni for help on behalf of the Strada Vini Valtellina; Paolo Ciaparelli, Gloria Maxenti and Albino Mazzolini of the Bitto Storico Centre for organising an unforgettable day with Michele Lombella and the herdsmen up in the summer pastures; Roger Marchi in the Oltrepò Pavese; Massimo Pirotta in Bellinzago Lombardo; Paolo and Nadia Gallini in Milan; Robert Griffin, my photographer and travel organising cousin who was savvy enough to make a Lombard restaurant recommendation — who knew? Dario Medde of Adrastea Viaggi in Tirano for friendly and efficient help with our Bernina Express trip; Aldo Palaoro for help in Milan; Cathy Colecchi for help, hand holding and the best raised eyebrow in NY; Abigail Huges-Jones for always being there; Martin Darlison of Encompass Graphics for reliably beautiful maps; the brilliant and adorable Anita Mangan who sprinkles creativity with laughter and "dancing" even in the midst of daft workloads — it was crazy and fun; and finally, Dan who went way beyond the call of duty and dedicated a huge amount of time and energy, often in very challenging circumstances to capturing the essence of the stories in his photographs. I am very grateful to you all.

The photographer would like to thank: All of the people featured in this book. My encounters with those who cultivate the fields, raise the animals, catch the fish, make the wine and cook and serve the food in Lombardy were unforgettable. Meeting and working, albeit fleetingly, with the Lombards in their kitchens, wineries, on their plains and hillsides was an enormous privilege and I am grateful to all who made my brief intrusions into their lives rewarding and enjoyable. And finally to Christine, the inspiration for this book — her boundless energy and dedication have opened my eyes to the culinary treasures and wonderful people of Lombardy.